GROSS DECEPTIVE PRODUCT

An ecological perspective on the economy

Think Sustainably!

Russ England

RUSSELL ENGLAND

ISBN 978-1-64003-789-2 (Paperback)
ISBN 978-1-64003-790-8 (Digital)

Covenant Books, Inc.
11661 Hwy 707
Murrells Inlet, SC 29576
www.covenantbooks.com

CONTENTS

Acknowledgments 5
Tail Tale 7
Introduction..9

Chapter 1: From Farmer to Ecologist.........................15
Chapter 2: The Economy 30
Chapter 3: Basic Ecology 44
Chapter 4: Environmentalism......................................57
Chapter 5: Sustainability 67
Chapter 6: Fueling Economic Growth 78
Chapter 7: Promoting Growth....................................92
Chapter 8: The Cost of Growth...............................108
Chapter 9: Expectations vs. Realities........................116
Chapter 10: Relearning Nature...................................129
Chapter 11: Rethinking Government 142
Chapter 12: Final Thoughts..159

Literature Cited...169

ACKNOWLEDGMENTS

My interest in elucidating the conflicts between economic growth and ecosystem issues stemmed primarily from my efforts as a fisheries biologist to protect aquatic systems from the smothering effects of soil erosion. Gradually over the course of a thirty-year career, I came to the conclusion that economic growth is not only the major threat to the world's ecosystems but it is, for many reasons, unsustainable in its own right. I am grateful to many co-workers and friends who gave me feedback and encouraged me to refine my ideas.

I owe thanks to various editors of the *Gainesville Times* and the *Atlanta Journal/Constitution* for publishing my opinion columns as guest editorials over several years. I am thankful for the many positive comments I received from the public as a result of those articles, which further encouraged me to express my views and to eventually consider putting my opinions in book form.

I owe special thanks to Lawrence E. McSwain, a former co-worker and biologist friend, who graciously reviewed my draft manuscript and offered detailed constructive criticism. Charles Salter, retired outdoor page writer for the *Atlanta Journal/Constitution* also reviewed the manuscript and made helpful comments.

Finally, I wish to thank my wife Pat for making suggestions about content and for offering encouragement along the way.

TAIL TALE

I give you the case of Sir Oliver Sneeze
Who ruled a kingdom of a thousand fleas.

His kingdom encompassed an old Airedale,
Stretching from nose to tip of tail.

And high on the tail from a throne of hair
Good King Oliver ruled with flair.

But the wag of the tail created a breeze
That became intolerable for the ruling fleas.

This did not bother King Oliver, you see.
He solved the problem by simple decree.

His command was entered in the royal log:
"Henceforth the tail shall wag the dog"

The end of the tale? No, there's more to it.
The incredible thing—the dog let him do it!

Russell England
c. 1980

Introduction

I recently stayed overnight in a motel room in a town in central Kentucky, where I picked up a magazine billed as a "guide for newcomers and visitors." It was interesting reading, and I suspect it is fairly representative of many other chamber of commerce–type publications produced around the country that are designed to promote economic growth in local areas.

The first page of text has the headline "Welcome to one of America's best small towns." Listed among the attributes of this town is a "vibrant business community supported by the active 275 member strong [town name] chamber of commerce and the economic development arm of the city government. The community has received numerous awards and recognitions from national and international publications, including being named one of America's Best Small Towns for several years."

The welcome page goes on to say that the city has a stable infrastructure and that "local government works to improve services and sustain an unmatched quality of life, while keeping cost of living low and economic growth sustainable." The city has single- and multi-family housing and commercial development available as well as a strong industrial community that provides employment across the region.

I will include additional quotes from this "small town" magazine that are relevant to the topic of this book. For example, the construction of an interstate highway in the 1960s brought "more growth and opportunity" and the town is billed as "a popular tourism stop as well as a place for new residents to find a welcoming home."

The county this town is in "is one of the fastest growing areas" in the state, but it "takes great pride in its small town atmosphere." The business community "is the vibrant and growing key to maintaining the city as a wonderful place to live." The chamber of commerce "works tirelessly to advance business" and promotes the town "as a place to live and work."

"In addition to the more conventional ways of luring industry and other big business, the city's economic development office is charged with not only recruiting and assisting new businesses and industries . . ., but also helping existing business improve and expand." The town's economy is already "supported by more than 3,500 industrial jobs."

"To make more room for industrial growth, the city" and its industrial development authority "expanded in 1996, purchasing 474 more acres." A new middle school has opened on fifty acres of the property and "other industries are being recruited to settle on the rest."

Now let me take the liberty of putting my own take on the message being advanced in the publication I just quoted from. My take on the publication comes from an ecological perspective rather than an economic one, but hopefully the reader will also recognize a good dose of common sense.

The town considers itself small and uses that notion in an attempt to make itself attractive to people who might be lured to visit or live there. And why would this town want to attract more people? Apparently, so it can grow to become a larger town. And it seems logical to ask how large does this "town" want to be? This question is not answered directly, but considering all the expense and effort aimed at attracting new industry and people and the fact that the town's governing body is working hard to make economic growth sustainable, one could logically conclude that the town really wants to keep growing forever, or at least until it becomes a large city. But many large cities also spend a lot of money trying to lure more growth, so I suspect the characterization that the town wants to grow forever is the most accurate.

Of course, the larger the "town" becomes, the less credible will be its claim to being attractive because it is a small town, so at some point it will have to come up with a different marketing ploy to sell itself. The magazine does not directly say that the town wants to grow in population, merely that it wants economic growth. But how can it not grow in population if it invites newcomers to live there and begs new industries to bring in new jobs? New jobs are not filled exclusively by people already living in the area; in fact, new jobs are often filled primarily by people moving in from outside who are more likely to already have the skills needed by the new industry. It seems clear that those who want economic growth recognize that population growth is a main driver of economic growth and is therefore very desirable from their point of view.

So what is the town's goal? It would appear that the goal is simply growth, with no thought given to what an optimum population density or economic condition might look like. This growth goal is not unique to this particular "small" town, but is ubiquitous throughout the nation among towns, cities, and even rural areas, regardless of the current population density or strength of the resource base. The city of Atlanta, with its extreme traffic congestion and insecure water source for its current population is a good example of the growth goal mind-set. It was recently reported in the local paper that the Atlanta chamber of commerce is spending $20 million to encourage millennials to move to the area.

The terms "growth," "opportunity," and "progress" are often used in various combinations to convey a positive message about economic outlook. I find it particularly interesting that the word "progress" is so often used to imply a beneficial condition even though there is no stated goal that is to be progressed toward. From an economic standpoint, progress and growth are often used interchangeably because without growth the economy is considered ailing and therefore not "progressing" toward a larger size or a more favorable circumstance. But is progress a meaningful term without a stated goal or end point to progress toward?

From an ecological perspective, it would seem that stability, and some optimum population level, are more reasonable goals than perpetual growth. The economy is only a manmade system of exchanging goods and services for one species and is therefore only a small portion of the ecosystem; it is not the other way around. The present paradigm, in which the desire for economic growth drives decision-makers to ignore ecological principles, seems to me a clear case of the economic tail wagging the ecosystem dog.

I have to wonder whether the chamber of commerce in the above referenced community represents the views of the average citizen. After all, the chamber has 275 members while the total population of the town was just over 14,000 people as of 2014. Granted, the city officials are elected, so theoretically the voters have a say in whether the city has an economic development arm that works with the chamber of commerce, but the choices before the voters at election time probably did not include a candidate that would question the wisdom of perpetual growth.

In this book, I wish to make it clear to the reader that economic growth is not sustainable over the long run. I have reached this conclusion because such growth depends on an ever-growing population, passing debt to future generations and the use of finite natural resources, many of which are being rapidly depleted and are not renewable. Economic health is currently measured by a nation's gross domestic product (GDP) and an economy that is not growing toward an ever-larger GDP is considered unhealthy. Any business that focused solely on gross sales and ignored net profits or losses would likely not last long. I hope to demonstrate to the reader why I believe that measuring a nation's economic health only in gross terms is inadequate when the net benefits or costs of growth are not taken into account.

Because of what I call the "grow or die" paradigm so prevalent in our modern society the idea that there might be some optimum human population density for a community, a nation, or the world for that matter, is rarely given any serious consideration. Such thinking does not consider the long-term consequences of growth and it is diametrically opposed to the ecological perspective that considers a healthy ecosystem as one in which there is a natural balance among living and nonliving things and where no one species is so dominant that it destroys or degrades its own environment or the environment of other species upon which it may depend.

CHAPTER 1

FROM FARMER TO ECOLOGIST

Growing up on small subsistence farms in northern Virginia, I learned early on that food does not originate in grocery stores. My family raised cattle, hogs, and chickens and harvested hay, corn, and wheat to feed them. We also grew a large variety of vegetables in our home garden. My mother delivered cream, butter, and eggs to regular customers in a nearby town on a weekly basis—a business she took over from her father when he was no longer able to do it. She also supplemented the family income by working part-time jobs at apple processing plants and as a switchboard operator for the local telephone company.

I learned the rigors and rewards of hard work. I remember some of my first chores were pulling and hoeing weeds in our home garden and picking potato beetles and their eggs off the leaves of potato plants. I soon learned to milk cows by hand (not as easy as it looks, but once you learn how it is like riding a bicycle—you never forget how). Most importantly, I learned not just how to do the various chores around the farm, but I began to take responsibility to see that some of the chores got done.

Life on the farm was not all work, however. I learned to enjoy hunting and fishing at an early age. My first hunting experience involved shooting English sparrows with a Daisy Red Ryder BB gun, almost a must-have accessory for a farm boy growing up where I did. My parents made it clear to me that songbirds were off limits; only English sparrows, European starlings, and pigeons were fair game. These three were considered pests around the farm because they ate grain meant for livestock and often placed their nests where they contributed to unsanitary conditions. I soon learned to distinguish among the various species of sparrows so I could be sure to target only the exotic English variety.

My first real gun was a Stevens .22 caliber single-shot bolt action rifle with open iron sights, a hand-me-down from my older brother, and with this rifle, I began working on the groundhog (woodchuck) populations on our farm and those of several neighbors. Groundhogs were considered pests because they ate crops and dug holes that posed a danger to livestock and farming equipment. I also hunted squirrels and rabbits in season and these experiences became the beginnings of a life-long interest in hunting. I also became quite proficient with firearms.

I learned to fish in small creeks and occasionally in the north fork of the Shenandoah River, which was only a few miles away. My grandfather sometimes took us fishing in the river for catfish at night, and my brother and I fished both in the daytime and at night in a small creek near my grandparents' farm. We would occasionally hook an eel; a unique experience because the eel would wrap its snake-like body around rocks and one had to just apply steady pressure until the eel tired and released its grip. I remember one day when I caught a fourteen-inch largemouth bass in that small creek. This was a real trophy catch for such a small stream and my brother, reluctant to have anyone see the fish and ask where we caught it, carried the fish home in one of his high-topped rubber boots. Catch and release fishing was unheard of in that day and age; everything we caught went into the frying pan.

When we weren't hunting or fishing, we were farming with horsepower, literally, and human power; we did not own a tractor until my brother bought a used John Deere after he graduated from high school. I can vividly recall plowing, mowing, and raking hay and hauling it unbaled to the barn, planting and cultivating corn, planting wheat—all with horses pulling the various equipment appropriate to the task. My father seemed to enjoy working with horses—it was in his blood, so to speak.

I can recall, as a boy of ten or so, watching a hired crew using a stationary threshing machine in my grandfather's barn to separate wheat from chaff. Within a few years, such machines were replaced by mobile combines going from farm to farm, cutting the wheat stalks, separating the grain and discharging the chaff in a neat row to be picked up later by a baler. The threshing machines, combines, and balers were of course powered by tractors, although now the tractor-drawn combines have long since been replaced by self-propelled machines.

My parents experienced firsthand the great depression; as a result they were thrifty and did not believe in borrowing money. They married late (my father was forty and my mom 30) and my father worked as a carpenter, fishing guide, and a farm manager for a wealthy landowner in Maryland before we moved to Virginia and lived for a few years with my mother's parents while they looked around in the area for a farm of their own. They finally found an eighty-acre farm with a sturdy house and barn and several outbuildings, for which they paid $12,500 cash from their savings. The farm was just a few miles from my grandparents' farm and we moved there during the summer before I entered sixth grade.

My first paying job that I can recall was mowing approximately two acres of property owned by the small country church my family attended. This included a cemetery and what seemed to me like a large open field that was apparently intended for future expansion of the cemetery. I was probably in about the seventh grade in school when I began this mowing job, and I can vividly remember my mom giving me lots of encouragement to keep at it in spite of my not always wanting to do it when the time came. This job turned out to be a great opportunity for me to learn responsibility for getting a job done and became a source of pride of accomplishment when the task was completed. It was also a great opportunity for me to begin saving money for future needs. I recall that I was paid $16 each time I mowed, a task that took two full days to complete.

Later on, I worked during summer vacations for a neighbor who had an orchard and some rental property.

I started out picking cherries for fifteen cents a gallon (I could pick about six gallons an hour if I really hustled and if the crop was good). Later, the neighbor hired me at $0.90 per hour to help spray his fruit trees, paint buildings and do other odd jobs. I remember painting the roof of a rental house with aluminum paint in the bright sunlight and in the middle of the summer—a hot task indeed!

Although my family's way of life seemed well-suited to me during my growing-up years, as I approached manhood, it seemed less and less like a viable way to make a living. With the advantage of hindsight, it is clear that the world was rapidly changing even back then. Subsistence farms were beginning to give way to retreats for the wealthy or housing developments and most young adults were leaving the farms for college or steady jobs in manufacturing or the service industries. Mechanization was rapidly changing even small farming practices, and I personally witnessed the horse-drawn equipment era drawing to a close. Outside of the Amish and Mennonite communities, it is rare to find people in the United States still farming with horses. It is even getting hard to find people who remember farming that way.

I went off to a small liberal arts college not knowing what I wanted to do with my life, but declared a major in mathematics, probably because algebra and geometry were my favorite subjects in high school and I did well in them. However, after a course in advanced algebra and trigonometry in my freshman year, I decided that math was not for me and switched my major to biology. This seemed like a good fit with my farming background and a seemingly innate interest in the plants and animals and the natural world around me.

In retrospect, it is clear to me why I initially chose math instead of biology as my major. I had good algebra and geometry teachers in high school who knew the subject matter well and were passionate about teaching. By contrast, the biology and chemistry teachers I encountered were simply not very competent and showed little interest in teaching. In college, my general chemistry professor approached the subject as if his students had had no chemistry in high school, which I greatly appreciated since my high school chemistry teacher had a habit of sleeping during labs, which says a lot about the quality of the course.

Having decided on biology as a college major, I began taking a variety of classes that put me on a course to graduate with a biology major and a chemistry minor. I enjoyed most of the required classes for my major, and I especially enjoyed a basic ecology class and an elective geology class which I found very interesting (and not just because that is where I met my future wife). I think it was late in my junior year of college that I began to think about a possible career in wildlife management.

Wildlife management also seemed like a good fit with my interests. I have already mentioned spending much of my leisure time during my youth fishing in small streams and hunting small game and woodchucks. The general ecology class taken as an undergraduate did much to clarify the interconnectedness of various life forms for me. I believe that course was a major factor in setting the direction my life was to take. I also found my classes in chemistry, geology, and ornithology interesting, although demanding. At no point do I remember asking myself what course of study would lead to the highest-paid career.

I applied to a couple of universities with reputable graduate programs in wildlife management and was offered a research assistantship in a newly established fisheries program at Virginia Tech. Although fisheries was not my first career choice, the assistantship was the major determining factor in my taking that fork in the road. Again, with the advantage of hindsight, that turned out to be a good decision.

At Virginia Tech, I took wildlife courses along with the few fisheries-related classes available in the fledgling fisheries program. After two years of study and completion of a thesis on the effects of runoff from abandoned manganese strip mines on the aquatic life in nearby streams, I earned a master of science degree in the spring of 1968. While the diploma said wildlife management, I felt I could rightfully claim to be Virginia Tech's first master's degree fisheries graduate.

While I was going to school, the military draft was still in existence, but as long as I stayed in college, I was able to get deferments. Once I finished my master's degree, however, I knew there was no point in looking for a full-time job because I had no doubt I would soon be drafted into the army. This was at a time before the lottery system of drafting was instituted; virtually every able-bodied young man was being drafted. I considered enlisting in a National Guard unit in an attempt to avoid the Vietnam War, but decided I did not want to spend more than two years in military service. Sure enough, in September 1968 I was drafted into the army.

My military experience began with basic training at Fort Bragg, NC. The training was rigorous and tough at times. We had a very demanding drill sergeant who pushed the company to win all the training awards given by the battalion (which we did). I felt like my early experience with outdoor activities and proficiency with firearms better prepared me for military training than was the case with many of my fellow trainees. I was able to help some of them with marksmanship and encourage others to get through the more demanding physical activities.

In addition to basic training at Fort Bragg, I went through advanced infantry training (AIT) at Fort Polk, LA (which didn't seem much different from basic). After AIT, I was fortunate to be selected for non-commissioned officer candidate school (NCOC) at Fort Benning, GA. Then I spent three months as a training NCO for the next NCOC class, which meant that the first year of my two-year military obligation was spent in the states. Inevitably though, I was shipped off to South Vietnam for my final year of service. I can still recall seeing the bomb-scarred landscape as the airplane approached the Saigon airport and wondering what I had gotten myself into.

In Vietnam, I spent a year as a platoon sergeant with the 199th Light Infantry Brigade patrolling an area of jungle southeast of Saigon. Fortunately, our assignment was in an area where there seemed to be no major enemy activity at the time. I was second in command of a platoon and spent one month of my year-long assignment as acting platoon leader. I am thankful that no one in my platoon was killed during my tenure in the field, although a few were seriously wounded.

I saw from the field level that the war was poorly managed and that winning did not seem to be the objective. There was a strong emphasis on body count, even to the point that field officers went out of their way to make the numbers look good—accurate or not, essentially telling their superiors what they wanted to hear. I remember that one month my platoon was cited for having the highest body count (twenty something as I recall) of any platoon in the brigade, and yet I had not seen the first body that we could honestly claim that our platoon had killed. The numbers included a half dozen fresh graves that we found and various other incidents when our commanding officer reported unverified kills based on what my platoon leader thought might have been.

One incident in particular stands out in my mind. After a brief firefight, our platoon cautiously approached a freshly-abandoned bunker complex. Our company commander was communicating via radio with his superior in a helicopter and, seeing red liquid on the side of a tree, assumed it was blood and reported it as a kill. I pointed out to him that the red liquid was not blood but was actually sap oozing out of bullet holes in the tree, but instead of correcting the mistake, he shrugged it off saying something like "oh well, we'll get credit for a kill." If this was the attitude throughout the war effort at the time, it is easy to see that the top commanders were receiving bad information relative to the success of the war even while getting the feedback from the field that they wanted to hear.

After leaving the army, and after several months looking for work, I was fortunate to get hired as a fisheries biologist with the state of Georgia's Game and Fish Commission. This agency soon became the Game and Fish Division of the Department of Natural Resources (DNR), which came into being with Governor Jimmy Carter's reorganization of state government shortly after I began work. I say I was fortunate because there were not many government agencies or private companies hiring fisheries biologists at the time I entered the job market, but also because this turned out to be a well-run agency that was, for the most part, a joy to work for.

My first assignment was as a trout biologist and my office was at a trout hatchery at the edge of Lake Burton, a Georgia Power Company hydroelectric reservoir in the mountainous northeastern corner of the state. I was responsible for completing on-going research projects on trout streams and planning new ones. I was also charged with overseeing a state trout hatchery and stocking trout from state and federal hatcheries into streams and lakes, and monitoring fish populations in nearby reservoirs operated by Georgia Power Company and the Tennessee Valley Authority. A smaller part of my job involved investigating reports of fish kills and pollution and writing environmental opinions about projects that could potentially impact trout waters.

I found the work fascinating and demanding. I had a lot to learn that I was not exposed to in school and had to re-learn much that I was rusty on after three years out of graduate school. I loved the work, though, and sometimes found it hard to believe that I was getting paid what many people with a master's degree would consider a meager salary for doing such interesting work.

As the years went by, I became increasingly involved in environmental issues. One of the first efforts in this regard was working with the US Forest Service in the mid-1970s to protect trout streams from excessive soil erosion resulting from timber harvesting activities. I can recall crossing a stream culvert in my car and seeing muddy water, then driving upstream on a gravel road to find the source. This turned out to be a bulldozer building a logging road and in the process actually pushing dirt into the stream in places. Upon interviewing the bulldozer operator and later talking with Forest Service engineers, I learned that an elaborate plan for the road had been prepared that specified such things as a buffer along the stream and where culverts and drainage structures would be placed, but the bulldozer operator had simply been told by his boss to "make a road so trucks could get the timber out." A classic example of the best laid plans being put on the shelf and not implemented.

I was also involved early on with the US Soil Conservation Service (now the Natural Resources Conservation Service) in efforts to stop stream channelization and the construction of flood control impoundments on trout waters. The typical SCS flood control impoundment had about twenty acres or less of permanent pool but the structure temporarily stored much more water during storm events. One of my projects was designed to monitor the effects of some of these impoundments on stream temperature and it involved the use of clock-wound thermographs to monitor stream temperatures upstream and downstream of the impoundments.

This study was labor-intensive in that it required someone to change the paper charts on the machines and check their calibration on a weekly basis and then record hourly temperature readings from the charts to be tabulated and analyzed by hand, as this was before the desktop computer age. The effort was worthwhile because it clearly documented the warming of water as it passed through the impoundments, even those designed to draw the coldest water from the bottom of the lake. That study, along with a previously passed law forbidding raising trout stream temperatures, did much to stop the Soil Conservation Service from building impoundments on trout waters in Georgia.

Of course, this study led to more work in the form of a permitting system for anyone wanting to build a farm pond or other small impoundment on trout waters. The permitting system was administered by the Environmental Protection Division of DNR, but it fell to fisheries biologists to review each application and make a recommendation as to whether to approve the permit. This process became an educational one for both the landowners and the biologists as it was often difficult to decide whether the proposed impoundment would have a significant impact on downstream temperatures and often just as difficult to explain to the landowner the rationale for the decision whether to approve or deny. Although landowners usually felt they owned the stream on their property and therefore could do with it as they pleased, in fact they only owned the stream bottom; by law the water in the stream and the aquatic life therein is owned by the state and therefore it fell upon DNR employees to protect the quality of the water and the fish and other aquatic species living there.

In 1976, Georgia passed the Erosion and Sedimentation Act, which established a twenty-five-foot vegetative buffer on each side of all state waters and a one-hundred-foot buffer on designated trout streams. With the exception of road construction, this act applied to practically all major land-disturbing activities, public or private. Development could take place inside the buffer zone only with a variance issued by the Environmental Protection Division (EPD) of DNR.

I soon began to observe apparent violations of the buffer requirements and sought help from EPD to enforce the rules. EPD, not having adequate staff to administer the buffer requirements, began sending me variance requests to review. I began making recommendations to issue or deny variances and gradually developed guidelines for a scientific approach to the analysis of variance requests, including recommendations for mitigation measures to be implemented as a condition for granting a variance. I tried to suggest mitigation measures that would result in no net negative impact on water quality, but often such measures did not seem practical in which case I would recommend denial of a variance. The process often involved difficult decisions, and needless to say, I didn't make many friends among land developers who had to deal with stream buffer issues.

As Georgia's population continued to increase, the northeastern region of the state became a hotbed for environmental issues, with increasing demands for streamside and lakeside development and new road construction. I got involved in investigating more frequent fish kills from a variety of causes, and in reviewing and commenting on a variety of projects that could negatively impact public waters. By the mid-1980s, it began to dawn on me that although an individual project might affect a stream in a relatively minor way, the cumulative effects of various projects would gradually alter the stream's ability to sustain the variety and abundance of fish species and other aquatic life that its unaltered state would support. A study by US Geological Survey biologists confirmed my beliefs, demonstrating that streams draining urban areas supported about half the number of fish species and half the overall quantity of fish compared to streams draining undeveloped watersheds.

About the same time, I began to notice a growing public concern about development projects that folks did not want "in their backyards." More and more people began to attend public meetings about proposed developments, and I began to hear statements that went something like this: "I'm not against growth, but this project will have a negative impact on my neighborhood and decrease the value of my property." Pro-growth people began to label folks who spoke out against individual projects as NIMBYS (not in my backyard), usually meaning it in a somewhat derogatory way.

Hearing more and more people speak out against single development proposals helped reinforce my growing realization that the problem was greater than the sum of the individual projects impacting the environment in their individual and often minor ways. I gradually reached the conclusion that the problem was really a result of society's firmly entrenched view that growth is good and must not only be accommodated but encouraged. It seemed to me that the only possible result of continuous growth would be to eventually negatively impact or perhaps destroy the quality of life for all of us.

It was sometime in the 1980s that I began educating myself on economic matters and seriously pondering the relationship between prevailing economic thinking and environmental concerns. It didn't take long for me to conclude there was a direct conflict between the over-arching economic paradigm that demands continuous growth and the basic ecological principles I had learned in college; principles such as carrying capacity (the number or weight of individuals that can be supported by a given quantity of habitat), species diversity, and how various species depend on each other and on nonliving things for their survival.

In subsequent chapters of this book, I will share my understanding of some general principles as they apply to ecology and economics and try to put forth a logical argument for why I believe economic growth as we know it today must be limited if we are to preserve the essential ecological services such as clean air and water and renewable raw materials that our planet provides. This book is not intended to be a scientific or academic work, but hopefully, it will be one that can be understood by readers from all walks of life. I have included a limited number of references to other works, but where I fail to cite references, the information is readily available on the internet if the reader wishes to verify what I have to say.

CHAPTER 2

THE ECONOMY

This chapter is labeled "The Economy" and not "Economics" because the economy is the result of various economic activities and is therefore the term more suitable for discussion within the context of this book. I do not need to go into detail (nor am I qualified to) about the science of economics to make my points, but I think it would help the reader to have some understanding of the history of economic thinking as I believe it relates to today's prevailing view of overall economic well-being. It may also help the reader to better understand later discussions of how that prevailing view relates to other sciences, especially the science of ecology.

Economics is often called the dismal science because it is based on the study of a system that can't possibly satisfy all wants and needs. Economists supposedly recognize the scarcity of resources and try to figure out how to allocate those resources to benefit the most people or to identify alternative resources that can be substituted for scarce ones. Thus the word *scarcity* is a central concept of the study of economics.

Even though the study of economics is in many ways centered around scarcity, the economy we recognize today would never have developed except for surpluses. Our prehistoric human ancestors apparently recognized that certain wild food-producing plants could be cultivated to enhance their productivity at least ten thousand years ago, but it took a very long time for agricultural practices to develop to the extent that individual "farmers" produced more food than they needed for their own existence. Thus it was agricultural surplus that enabled diversification of means of making a living, trade of goods or services for that surplus, and eventually money to develop as a medium of exchange. The development of money allowed a standard way of measuring economic activity and eventually enabled the science of economics to evolve.

The science of economics began to materialize during a time when draft animals and human sweat provided most of the power to produce goods and services. Having grown up on a farm that depended on horsepower I can readily relate to that era. The first identifiable theory of economics was known as physiocracy (derived from Greek and meaning "government of nature") and is attributed to a group of eighteenth-century Frenchmen who believed that all wealth came from agriculture. These physiocrats argued that productive labor is the sole source of a nation's wealth and their line of reasoning replaced the idea of mercantilism, which held that the value of products for a society was created at the point of sale, and focused on the ruler's wealth, accumulation of gold and a favorable balance of trade.

The physiocrats saw farmers and others who worked in agriculture as the ultimate producers. Tradesmen such as leather workers, bakers, and clothiers contributed to the economy only by making products from agricultural surplus. Merchants were seen as people who bought and sold for a profit, and while they contributed services by distributing goods to those who could afford it, the physiocrats did not consider them part of the economy.

The Scottish philosopher Adam Smith recognized growth as it relates to economic activity, but he believed that economic growth would eventually have limits based on the nature of a nation's soil and climate. His 1776 book *An Inquiry Into the Nature and Causes of the Wealth of Nations* is considered the first significant written work on economics. Even today Smith is regarded as one of the most influential thinkers in the field and is often called the father of the science of economics. In his day, Smith was considered a moral philosopher and his early thinking on economic matters dealt with political economy, a term used for studying issues of production, trade, laws, customs, and governments of individual countries (polities) and how income and wealth was distributed. Thus the field of economics was closely related to politics from its very beginnings and it certainly remains so today.

Adam Smith predicted the world's economy could grow for about two hundred more years before natural limits were reached. Although this was way too far in the future for him to address in his writings in more than a speculative manner, it seems a rather accurate prediction from the perspective of those of us who believe we recognize signs that we are living in a full world today. By a full world, I mean full in the sense that the activities of human populations are significantly degrading the earth's resources and thus its ability to provide essential ecological services such as clean air and water and unadulterated food. Since many of those same resources that have supported ecological services also have supported economic activity, it seems logical that their degradation likely means that natural limits for the economy are being reached as well.

Thomas Malthus, an English cleric and scholar, is well known for predicting that human population would ultimately grow beyond the capacity of its food supply to sustain it. His predictions grew out of a realization that population had the potential to increase at an exponential rate and his belief that food production could only increase in a linear fashion. In 1805, Malthus became the first professor of political economy in the English-speaking world. He was a prolific writer who stressed the importance of the long-term stability of the economy over short-term advantage.

Although he was right about rates of population increase, Malthus could not have foreseen the dramatic increases in agricultural production that came about during the next two centuries. He still may be proven correct in predicting the world's population will outstrip its food supply. Localized famines have certainly occurred many times in different parts of the world, even in recent history, in spite of spectacular increases in food production and the development of advanced methods of storage, preservation and distribution (supported largely by depleting both fossil fuels and underground aquifers). Enormous challenges are facing the agricultural industry in feeding the world's projected population over the next few decades and many serious distribution problems remain to be solved.

So we see that the founders of the science of economics were long-term broad-thinking individuals who seemed to understand at least the theoretical limits of economic growth. How did we get away from their classical economic thinking to the prevailing "neoclassical" economics of today which rests on the widely-held assumption that growth has no limits and growth itself is a worthy and even necessary policy goal? I believe that part of the answer to that question lies in the industrial revolution that was just getting underway when Smith and Malthus were developing their ideas. Before discussing the changes brought about by the industrial revolution, however, let's take a brief look at the role that capitalism itself played in economic growth.

There are many types of economic systems; the three most familiar to the readers of this book are probably capitalism, socialism, and communism. By economic system, I mean the manner in which it is decided what products and how much to produce, how to produce the products, and how and to whom to distribute what is produced. Individual nations directly or indirectly choose their economic systems, based largely on the politics of those in control or on the nation's constitutional or legal constraints. Economic systems are generally considered either market economies, in which the market itself decides the above issues, or planned economies, where a central government makes most of those decisions. The economies familiar to Smith and Malthus were largely market economies and most of today's economic systems are either primarily or at least partially market-driven.

Most modern economists would likely argue that capitalism is the engine that drives economic growth. This is primarily because capitalism is based on private ownership of land and resources and thus the means of production and the freedom to make decisions that promote individual profit are in the hands of individual citizens. Prices for goods and services and distribution of these are determined primarily by competition and other factors such as supply and demand for individual products. Individual freedom and competition lead to innovation, which in turn lead to increased productivity and technological advances far beyond what can be expected in planned economies where individuals have less freedom to make decisions and have little incentive to produce more than expected.

While capitalism may be the engine of economic growth, the factors that fuel the growth engine are capital, labor, and productivity. Capital describes the financial resources to pay for wages, machinery, and other things needed to produce goods or services. Capital can take the form of cash from savings or investments or borrowed money (debt). Labor of course is the combined effort of individual workers who produce the goods or services. Productivity means the quantity of goods or services produced per worker. So for an economy to grow in size, one or more of these three things must be increasing. More on this thought later, but for now, let's return to the earlier thought about how the industrial revolution helped bring about the current thinking that an ever-growing economy is vital to economic health.

As the industrial revolution got underway, economists began to recognize that technological advances would increase not only agricultural efficiency but the overall efficiency of economic activity as well. As the industrial revolution progressed, it was also discovered that economic growth could depend on increasingly efficient power sources. So fueling the economy progressed from muscle power (either human or draft animal) to water power to wood to coal to oil and so forth. As one source of mechanical power was tapped out or became insufficient to meet the needs of industry another more efficient source was discovered and harnessed, thus the concept of substitutability was recognized by economists. While common sense would suggest that substitution of one fuel source with another more efficient one is not likely to go on forever it still appears to be a prominent concept in economic thought.

Common sense would also imply that efficiency of production cannot increase forever, at least not without undesirable consequences. For example, the more machines are able to take over repetitive tasks, the more human laborers find themselves unemployed. Try to visualize a theoretical extreme condition where all manufacturing and all service tasks are done by robots. In such a scenario, who would have the opportunity to live a productive life except those few who know how to repair the robots when they break down, or perhaps a few government employees? And there would be little money to pay government employees because robots don't pay taxes. To some extent, we are already living in a world where robots and computers have replaced so many workers that only those with special skills or the right connections can readily find the most gratifying employment.

As technology became ever more sophisticated, it also became more in demand and more newsworthy. The American public increasingly became enthralled with and supported a market for things new and innovative, especially if they enriched their lives and made their lives more enjoyable. People turned increasingly to debt to finance their wants and needs while government policy often encouraged debt by policies such as making home mortgage interest payments tax deductible and reducing the fraction of assets that banks were required to hold in reserve. Governments at all levels set examples that encouraged a buy-now-pay-later mind-set with various types of deficit spending.

Thus it became easy for the average person to associate improving living standards with what economists were touting as economic growth. As long as payments could be made on the debt that supported these higher standards of living, it was generally seen as good economics for everyone. Economic growth thus became recognized by the general public, at least in free-market economies, as synonymous with personal well-being.

Keep in mind that technological advances in the developed world were beginning to take place during a time when physical frontiers were also readily available for expansion. Land was readily available for subdividing for new housing to accommodate a growing population. Improved farming methods allowed farmers to cultivate crops on land previously considered marginal for production. Many people were and still are making good money in the real estate and building industries, contributing further to the notion that economic growth is a good thing.

Of course, much of the public is enamored with growth because they readily see that it directly or indirectly benefits them financially. Growth generally drives up the price of real estate because of increased competition for a finite resource. People who own real estate thus come to expect its value to rise so they can sell it for a profit at some future date. Even farmers notice that growth drives up the value of their land and many see that as the basis of their future retirement program. It is easy to see why politicians who promise to grow the economy by attracting new industry and creating jobs get elected.

A very real downside to the ever-increasing cost of land is the concurrent increase in the cost of goods and services which need land in order to be produced. The rising land values likewise lead to increased cost and decreased availability of affordable housing, which in turn generally impacts the poorest citizens the most. These are also the very people who see their wages stagnate as a result of competition for low-paying jobs that become scarcer as large chain retailers replace small businesses and technological advances replace more workers with machines. In a nutshell, those who are fortunate to own land that becomes more valuable with growth get rewarded while those less fortunate may face an increasing struggle to eke out a living. But even the poor are likely to find the politician's promise to create jobs alluring because it helps keep alive their hopes for a better-paying job.

Thus the prevailing view of today's economy is that it must be constantly growing in order to be healthy. Governments make considerable effort to estimate economic output, unemployment rates, and other indicators of economic health as it relates to growth. Laws are often passed or policies put into effect that are specifically designed to keep the economy growing and to prevent a recession (a business cycle contraction loosely defined as a significant drop in economic activity spread over more than a few months) or a depression (a severe or prolonged recession lasting several years).

In the United States, the Federal Reserve System acts as a national bank, charged among other things with regulating the supply of money in circulation and, believe it or not, with maintaining the value of the dollar (which now buys maybe 5 percent of what it bought when the Federal Reserve began operating in 1914). The Federal Reserve is also responsible for monitoring the affairs of and auditing the records of all banks in its system, including twelve separate district banks and twenty-five regional branches scattered throughout the nation. Nearly all US banks are part of the Federal Reserve System, which requires that they maintain a certain percentage of their assets on deposit with a regional branch bank (this varies with net bank transactions but was no more than 10 percent as of 2015). Most other nations also have national banks that oversee their monetary and economic policies.

According to its mission statement, the US Department of Commerce (DOC) "promotes job creation, economic growth, sustainable development, and improved standards of living for all Americans . . ." (www.commerce.gov). In order to measure economic health it tracks leading economic indicators, including retail sales, new construction, manufacturing activity, and personal income among other statistics. The DOC also promotes "progressive business policies that help America's businesses and entrepreneurs and their communities grow and succeed." Notice the implication that all communities must grow to be successful, no matter how large or congested they already are or what their resource constraints may be. Notice also how the word "progressive" is associated with growth and success; implying good without considering the possibility that growth may have its downsides. The DOC is a shining example of the economy's connection to politics.

The usual measure of economic activity within a country is the gross domestic product (GDP). GDP is defined as the sum total of the gross market value of all goods and services produced within a country over a given time period. Put another way, GDP is a function of the total number of workers and their productivity. Productivity of course varies greatly from country to country, largely because of differences in access to technology. For example, a textile worker using an electrically powered loom produces much more finished material in a given amount of time compared to one using a loom powered by his or her hands and feet.

The health of a nation's economy is measured in terms of how its GDP grows or shrinks. A growing economy, one with an increasing GDP, is generally considered a healthy economy. All other things being equal, GDP can rise by increasing the number of workers or by increasing productivity of existing workers. Increasing productivity often means increasing dependence on fossil fuels, while increasing the number of workers generally means increasing the overall population or putting to work unemployed workers from the existing population. It seems clear to me that a growing economy, whether it depends on greater use of fossil fuels or on population increase, is unsustainable in the long run. If this is true, then some new and better way of measuring economic health is badly needed.

Relatively new to economic thinking is the field of environmental economics (www.epa.gov/environmental-economics), which is concerned with the efficient allocation of natural resources. A central concept of environmental economics is that markets fail to allocate resources in a manner that results in the greatest societal benefit. For example, what a private person or company decides to do based on market prices may be at odds with what the general public deems necessary to protect the environment. Environmental economists advocate the study of the costs and benefits of alternative environmental policies to deal with such things as toxic waste disposal, air pollution, and water quality. Such thinking is based on the premise that if one person becomes better off economically for making a business decision no other person should be worse off as a result of that one person's action.

Environmental economists recognize that the way the economy is managed affects the health of the environment, which in turn affects the performance and health of the economy. This thinking in turn recognizes that the economy and the environment are not separate entities but are dependent upon each other. The environment provides the raw materials needed for economic activity as well as direct values such as clean air to breathe and water to drink. While this is an important concept for economic thinking, it does not necessarily recognize the finite nature of natural resources nor does it question the need for continuous growth.

There is also a small but growing movement within the field of economics that believes that perpetual growth is neither possible nor desirable and folks involved in this movement are working to develop sound theories for a steady state economy. This movement, also known as ecological economics (www.steadystate.org), is trying to incorporate the basic principles of ecology (especially the earth's carrying capacity for humans) into mainstream economic thinking. While environmental economics recognizes the interdependence of the environment and economy, ecological economics goes a step further by proclaiming that the economy is actually a subset of the ecosystem and therefore subject to limitations imposed by ecological principles. Ecological economics emphasizes the protection of the natural capital provided by the ecosystem and rejects the notion that man-made capital can be substituted for natural capital.

Ecological economics has had trouble getting the recognition it needs to be given serious consideration by mainstream economists and political thinkers, perhaps for two reasons. First of all, it is a movement begun primarily by ecologists and environmental economists, folks who came from a perspective quite different from that of traditional economists and were therefore considered outsiders. Secondly, and perhaps more important, the "steady state economy" that is the central premise of ecological economics, starkly contradicts the "grow or die" paradigm that is so firmly entrenched in main-stream economic thinking.

For the time being there seems to be little chance that main stream economic thought will seriously consider any challenge to the entrenched idea that growth is vital to economic health or the overall well-being of humanity. Perhaps it will take another "great depression" and/or an unprecedented environmental disaster to significantly alter the status quo.

CHAPTER 3

BASIC ECOLOGY

The generally accepted definition of *ecology* considers it a branch of biology (the study of living things) that deals with the study of how living creatures interact with one another and with nonliving things in their physical surroundings or environment. The word *ecology* was derived from the Greek *oikos* (which literally means a place to live) and was coined by Ernst Haeckel, a German biologist, in 1869.

In its modern form, ecology is a relatively new science (dating from about 1900), although its complex origin can be traced to philosophers of ancient Greece (fourth and fifth centuries BC). Aristotle and Hippocrates began to record their observations on natural history as it related to physical characteristics of individual species. Aristotle studied animal behavior, migration, and physiology, all of which are part of modern ecological studies.

Although ecology as a science is considered new, it is reasonable to assume that the concept of studying interactions among species and their environments dates back to the dawn of civilization or even before. For example, prehistoric humans as a group must have been well-versed about where (what type of environment) and when (what season to harvest) to look for various types of food-producing plants and what parts of those plants were edible. They would also have been well aware of animal behavior, including migration routes and patterns that would contribute to their success as hunters. They would have known which animals were the most practical to pursue for food and which were most likely to eat them; in other words, they would have had a great deal of knowledge of what ecologists now call predator/prey relationships. They would also have known where to find the best water to drink and the best shelter to protect them from the elements.

Modern humans have essentially forgotten most of this "ecological" wisdom that their ancient (and even fairly recent) ancestors painstakingly accumulated over thousands of generations. Most of us who live in developed countries have only a vague idea of where and how the products we depend on for our survival are actually produced. Thus the study of the science of ecology can help us modern humans regain lost knowledge and better understand our environment and how it affects us and how we affect it. For the purpose of this book, it is necessary only to highlight some basic principles of ecology.

The concept of the ecological system, or ecosystem, is a fundamental principle of ecology. An ecosystem can be defined as a geographic area containing living organisms such as plants and animals plus nonliving components such as soil, water and air interacting in a way that results in an exchange of materials between the living and non-living parts of the system. As the basic functional unit in ecology, examples of ecosystems can range from the very small and ephemeral (such as a pool of water maintained by a seasonal wet-weather spring) or large and permanent (such as an ocean or a mountain range).

Whether you think of an ecosystem as simple or complex the overall concept itself is very broad. The take home message of the concept is to emphasize such principles as cause and effect, interdependence of species, and binding relationships among living and nonliving elements. In a sense, the whole earth could be considered an ecosystem, but the term "biosphere" is usually preferred when considering life at that scale. The biosphere actually makes up a relatively small portion of the whole earth since life only exists in a thin shell extending a relatively short distance down below the surface and up into the atmosphere. Within the biosphere, it is convenient and practical to consider individual ecosystems such as rain forests, deserts, grasslands, oceans, etc.

A typical ecosystem is composed of producers, consumers, decomposers, and nonliving substances or factors that support the first three. The most common category of producers is represented by the green plants which use sunlight, carbon dioxide, water, and essential minerals to manufacture or produce the food that supports their growth and development. Consumers (think animals) do not produce their own food but must depend on the consumption of plants or other animals for their nourishment. Decomposers are those organisms (primarily bacteria and fungi) that break down the complex material of dead plants or animals into simple compounds or molecules that can be used by producers. Finally, the nonliving (or abiotic) substances include such things as soil, water, sunlight, and air.

Not all ecosystems contain all four components mentioned above. For example, many areas at the bottoms of deep lakes and seas lack producers because of the lack of sunlight but such systems are sustained by a constant supply of organic materials settling by gravity from near the surface. But even some deep-sea areas may contain producers in the form of bacteria that are able to use chemicals such as sulfur, ammonia, or methane to produce biomass without the benefit of sunlight.

The concepts of habitat and niche are also important to the understanding of ecosystems. A basic definition of habitat is simply where an organism or species lives, or where you would go to find it. For example, if you were looking for wild (not stocked) brook trout in the southern Appalachians you would look in small high-altitude streams where very few or no other species of fish live. In a broader sense, habitat must include food supply, shelter and any other essentials for survival. That small stream ecosystem that provides brook trout habitat also supports aquatic insects (food) and contains gravel spawning areas and rocks and other debris where the trout can hide from predators.

The term *niche*, on the other hand, refers to what an organism does for a living and how it interacts with other species and its surroundings. In the case of the brook trout, it survives by feeding primarily on aquatic insects and terrestrial insects that fall into the water, thus the terms "consumer" and "predator" would help describe its niche. In simple terms, habitat can refer to an organism's address while niche would refer to how it makes its living.

A species may be adaptable to a wide variety of habitats or it may be limited to very narrow and specific habitat requirements. Some species can modify their surroundings to create the habitat they need. The beaver, for example fells trees and builds dams to flood meadows so that it can create a more secure environment to build its lodge and enable better access to its food supply. Its habitat modifications may have relatively short-lived results; once its food supply is depleted and its lake fills with sediment it will have to move on to find another place to build a dam.

Of course, man is the ultimate environment modifier with his ability to build and operate huge machines that can totally rearrange whole landscapes. He turns vast forests into farm or ranch land, digs large pits, or removes mountaintops for mining operations and moves massive amounts of dirt and rock to build highways, railroads, and canals. He dams rivers to create impoundments to control flooding, store drinking water, enhance navigation, generate electrical energy and create recreation areas. He builds solid homes, commercial buildings, airports—you name it. Indeed, man's ability to modify entire landscapes can be likened to a geologic force. Compared to the work of beavers, man's environmental modifications are permanent, unless you consider them in the context of geologic time.

Anytime one species modifies its environment to better its own survival it results in negative impacts on other species, and no other species can compare with humans when it comes to having adverse effects on others. Fortunately, humans have the ability to recognize at least some of the harm they do to other species and have taken a few steps to mitigate that harm. In the United States, the Endangered Species Act (ESA) has drawn attention to species that may be struggling to survive, and this struggle is often the result of loss of habitat due to human activity but it may also be due mainly to the fact that the species had very limited habitat all along. Either way, the ESA provides a limited mechanism for preventing or at least postponing the extinction of some species and, perhaps more importantly, for calling attention to potential problems associated with extinctions.

A species' niche, or how it makes its living, also plays a major role in how adaptable it is to its environment. A carnivore that feeds only on a few prey species or an herbivore that feeds only on a few types of plants is not going to be nearly as adaptable as an omnivore that feeds on a wide variety of plants and animals. For example, the giant panda and the koala feed almost exclusively on bamboo and eucalyptus, respectively. For either of these iconic species the destruction of a single type of plant could spell doom. Adaptability can therefore be an essential key to survival if habitat is altered and niche can be a key to adaptability or lack thereof.

Now unlike giant pandas or koalas, we humans are not totally dependent on a single species for our food supply. However, we are probably more dependent than most people realize on a very few species of plants to feed our vast numbers around the globe. Corn, for example, and to a lesser extent, wheat, soybeans, and rice represent by far the bulk of the plant species that supply our food either directly through the bread and cereal we eat or indirectly by feeding the cattle, hogs, poultry, and even fish that we eat. I will also mention here the rubber tree, without which our transportation system could not function as it does today, as an example of dependence on a single species.

The rubber tree is a native of South America, where it grows scattered throughout the rain forest. Those who attempted to grow the tree in densely populated monoculture situations in its native environment soon discovered that a fungus rapidly spread from tree to tree and killed every one before they could produce rubber. Henry Ford notably lost millions of dollars on a huge rubber plantation that he established early in the twentieth century. To get around the problem rubber plantations have been established in Asia where the deadly fungus does not exist. However, if the fungus ever gets a foot hold in the Asian plantations, the rubber industry is likely to crash. It is not far-fetched to envision such a scenario; we have seen many exotic species spread around the world (usually unintentionally) with very damaging results.

Carrying capacity is another fundamental concept of ecology and in its simplest form refers to the number of individuals of a given species that can be supported by its environment. The concept can be further divided to denote optimum or maximum carrying capacity. As one might guess, optimum carrying capacity would likely be less than maximum and would suggest individuals in good health, with plenty of food, and having some level of cushion against disruptions to the environment. In contrast, at maximum carrying capacity, much of a population would suffer from shortages and be likely to degrade its environment through overuse of resources, which would further reduce carrying capacity. In other words, optimum carrying capacity suggests a sustainable condition while maximum capacity denotes a population at the upper limits of its environment's capability to support it, making it subject to collapse if minor disruptions occur.

If carrying capacity is exceeded a species must adapt by consuming less or finding more resources or see its population reduced. In typical animal populations, exceeding carrying capacity results in malnutrition, increased predation of weakened individuals, greater susceptibility to diseases, or even starvation. In such incidences, the habitat is usually degraded and the population may be forced to drop well below the previous carrying capacity until the environment can recover.

Carrying capacity can also be thought of in terms of long term and short term. For example, climate fluctuations or weather patterns may have short-term positive or negative impacts on carrying capacity, due to changes in food supply for example, but have little influence in the long term. Long-term carrying capacity depends heavily on sustainable resources and lack of environmental degradation. The elimination of the American chestnut from eastern forests due to an exotic fungus greatly reduced the long-term carrying capacity for many species of wildlife that depended on the chestnut for their major source of winter food. The loss of the chestnut, which was the dominant forest tree throughout most of its range, was also a major economic blow to the human species due to the loss of a highly prized wood.

The principle of limiting factors is also an important ecological concept. The principle basically says that a living thing cannot exist in an abundance greater than that in which its least abundant requirement is available to support it. For example, the yield of a farmer's field may be limited by nutrient deficiencies in the soil. The farmer may be able to solve this problem by adding the correct amount and kind of fertilizer, but if he is poor perhaps he cannot afford the fertilizer so then his lack of money or trading material becomes the practical limiting factor.

In natural situations it is easiest to think of limiting factors in simple terms. We all know that most animals (including humans) require food, water, and some kind of shelter from the elements and/or from predators in order to grow and reproduce. If food is scarce for any given population its numbers will remain low regardless of how much water and shelter is available. Limiting factors may be seasonal; for example a white-tailed deer population may be limited by the amount of nuts produced by oak trees if there is little else to sustain it through the winter months.

Plants need large amounts of carbon dioxide, water and sunlight to grow and in most areas of the world these are readily available. For maximum production, plants also need soil that is rich in elements such as nitrogen, phosphorous and potassium. But soil scientists have identified some thirteen additional elements that are needed in small quantities for healthy plant growth. A soil that lacks an essential minor element such as boron or zinc may not support a decent crop, thus the minor element becomes a limiting factor.

Ranges of tolerance can also be thought of as limiting factors, although the concept is a bit different. Many fish species (trout for example) require cold water which restricts these fish to high latitudes, high elevations, spring-fed water bodies, or some combination of these that maintain cold temperature during the critical hottest months of the year. Tropical fish, on the other hand, are restricted to mid-latitude areas where water stays warm year round. Soil pH is a factor limiting the growth of plants; some plants (blueberries for example) need a very acid soil to thrive, while most food crops prefer a neutral to only slightly acid soil.

The main point that needs to be made here is that there is no reason to think that human beings are not subject to the same ecological principles as other organisms. Humans depend on other species and nonliving elements for their survival. Human populations require suitable habitat, are subject to limiting factors, and ultimately their numbers are restricted by the carrying capacity of their environment. Ecology as it pertains to humans is, in the final analysis, the study of an animal population and how it relates to its environment.

While basic ecological principles apply to human populations, there are unique characteristics that make human populations different from all others. Mankind's ability to modify his environment, his highly variable behavior and his development of culture extend far beyond that of other species. These traits have given modern humans the unprecedented capability to dominate other species and to a large extent determine whether many other species survive or become extinct.

The subject of mankind's dominance over other species and his surroundings is worthy of some discussion because it is easy to assume that this dominance is complete when in fact it is far from it. The degree to which man dominates and controls his environment is hard to measure, although the concept can be readily understood in a general way. For example, man can modify the earth's landscape by using heavy earthmoving equipment, drainage pipes, concrete, and so forth. Such landscape manipulation may have far reaching effects by changing storm water runoff patterns and causing flooding downstream. Such landscape changes often accelerate soil erosion and may even alter the chemical nature of natural streams and lakes, which may in turn reduce the ability of those waters to support fish populations and other aquatic life.

Air-conditioning is a good example of how man has been able to control his local indoor climate to make life bearable where outdoor climate is literally too hot to live and work comfortably. This ability to cool indoor areas has played a major role in fostering population growth in the southern US and in many other warm climates in the developed world. Air-conditioning, however, has its limits and does not prevent heat waves or droughts. Also, the burning of fossil fuels to generate electricity is unsustainable and creates air pollution problems that are not yet fully understood.

I mentioned that mankind, like other species, is subject to ecological limits such as carrying capacity. There is no easy way to calculate the earth's human carrying capacity and any attempt to do so needs to consider such things as period of time considered and what standard of living is acceptable. One must understand that carrying capacity over the short term (decades) is likely much larger than could be sustained over the long term (centuries). Over the short term, food crops can be sustained with groundwater irrigation and fertilizers mined or manufactured from fossil fuels, but many large aquifers are being rapidly depleted and chemical fertilization certainly has its limits.

Any attempt to calculate long-term carrying capacity as it applies to humans must consider how long essential natural resources can last or what substitutes can be found before those natural resources are depleted. If one assumed that long-term carrying capacity depended solely on the ability of renewable resources to maintain a moderate standard of living then it seems likely that the earth's current human population is well above maximum capacity.

I have heard it argued on talk radio shows that the earth has nowhere near reached its human carrying capacity because, for example, the entire existing world population could fit within the state of Texas. This is a silly argument, but some people seem to take it seriously. The fact that everyone could fit into a land area the size of Texas says nothing about the ability of our planet's natural resources to sustain them. For that matter, the world's current population would fit in the state of Rhode Island, with each person having about four square feet of space. So what? Such statements are irrelevant to carrying capacity.

It is important to understand that, from an ecological perspective, mankind is a consumer. As a consumer, mankind depends on producers for his livelihood. Man cannot produce his own food but must depend on green plants fueled by sunlight, water, and soil nutrients to provide that food for him. The food supply that supports the current human population is supported by technology that depends heavily on natural resources such as petroleum, natural gas, and water to boost the production of green plants to support man's consumption. Those natural resources exist in finite quantities and it is well known that many of them are being rapidly depleted.

I mentioned the beaver as an example of an animal that modifies its environment to suit its needs for food and shelter. While the beaver's habitat modifications adversely affect some species, its dams also create habitat for many others. Therefore, the beaver is sometimes called a keystone species because many other species depend on its small impoundments for their survival. Conversely, there is no reason to think that man is a keystone species. Indeed, because his activities tend to destroy more habitat for other species than they create, most of the earth's other creatures would likely get along fine without us.

CHAPTER 4

ENVIRONMENTALISM

Environmentalism, or the environmental movement, is a concept that has slowly evolved, beginning mainly in Western Europe and the United States and gradually spreading to other parts of the world, primarily those areas where there is sufficient wealth to lift much of the population out of extreme poverty and where there are widespread educational opportunities. In other areas, poverty forces a hand-to-mouth existence; as of 2015, about 20 percent of the world's 7.3 billion people lived on an income of less than a dollar a day, according to United Nations statistics.

Where abject poverty is the norm, the environment is often severely degraded due to overpopulation and the resulting competition for basic resources such as firewood and clean water makes these basic needs difficult to obtain. People living in such areas spend their days struggling to find and prepare their next meal and thus have little or no time or incentive to think about the quality of their environment or how to improve it. Lack of education is often cited as a major factor in limiting people's ability to understand the environmental consequences of their actions, but people who are mired in poverty often have no access to education or simply cannot afford it.

The industrial revolution began in relatively wealthy countries, and it was fueled by unprecedented consumption of coal, which in turn, resulted in high levels of smoke pollution in the atmosphere, especially in urban areas where the factory jobs were located. Chemical discharges from various industries combined with untreated human waste began to pollute waterways beyond their capacity to assimilate or absorb them.

It was not long before people began to realize that aquatic life was being severely impacted or destroyed by the raw discharges of chemicals and sewerage and that air quality was being severely degraded. Gradually, the urban middle class began to use its political power to bring about positive changes. The Alkali Acts passed by the British Parliament in 1863 to regulate air pollution from factories producing soda ash were among the first of modern environmental laws.

The environmental movement to protect air and water quality went hand in hand with the conservation movement to protect natural resources such as forests and wildlife. The conservation movement was based on ethical principles, including a recognition that man's activities could damage the environment, that humans have a responsibility to maintain environmental quality for future generations and that resource management should be based on sound science.

Early environmentalists such as Aldo Leopold and Henry David Thoreau began to observe and write about the impacts of man's actions on the local environments they were familiar with. Early environmental actions in the United States were mostly limited to establishing parks and setting aside natural areas to protect them from development. Later, especially after the 1962 publication of Rachael Carson's *Silent Spring* (which sold over two million copies) highlighted the dangers of pesticides, the environmental movement expanded to include regional and national issues. National media attention to high profile events, especially as seen through television, did much to educate the general public about environmental issues.

Perhaps the best example of events that spurred the environmental movement in the United States had to do with a series of at least thirteen fires that broke out on the Cuyahoga River in northeastern Ohio beginning as early as 1868. The river section between Akron and Cleveland was so polluted that fish could not survive. A fire in June 1969 caught the attention of *Time Magazine*, which described the river as oozing rather than flowing and in which a person "does not drown but decays."

In the United States, the expanded environmental movement has resulted in national legislation such as the Clean Air Act (1963), the National Environmental Policy Act (1970) and the Endangered Species Act (1973) to name some of the more high-profile laws. Along with national legislation a number of federal agencies have been established to administer and enforce these laws.

States have passed their own environmental laws and set up their own agencies to administer them, often in response to federal mandates or to avoid federal intervention in what many would consider state matters. These laws and regulations have resulted in cleaner streams and much improved air quality. Many other nations have adopted the US model to establish their own air and water quality control laws.

Individual people, at least those in developed nations, respond to environmental issues at different levels of interest and awareness. Even in developed nations many residents are living from hand to mouth and have little time for or interest in environmental issues. Many others live their lives primarily indoors and give little thought to where their food and other living essentials come from or what happens to their waste (unless sanitation workers go on strike for example). If encouraged or forced to recycle by their local government those with little awareness of their environment may come to view their recycle bins as having something to do with "protecting the ecology" but they probably do not have much understanding of ecology itself.

As awareness of environmental issues increases, either through media coverage or direct involvement with localized impacts of industry on air or water quality, a segment of the population begins to get involved, perhaps by joining "environmental groups" or taking action such as writing letters to the local newspaper or complaining to politicians. Often such action is in response to NIMBY issues where people are concerned about the impacts of a nearby project on their quality of life, whether it be a perceived or actual threat to air or water quality, or simply not wanting the increased traffic a new subdivision or industrial complex will bring to their neighborhood. Or their objection to a project may have nothing to do with the environment; it may just be a concern about the project's impact on property values.

At a higher level of environmental awareness, people tend to join groups with more wide-ranging agendas and get more involved in political action to lobby for clean air or water or protection of endangered species at the national level. Most of the national or international groups concentrate on fairly narrow issues, such as marine environments impacted by discarded fishing gear or plastic waste, protecting elephants or other large mammals from poaching, or nuclear proliferation just to name a few examples.

Let me take a paragraph to address a few pet peeves of mine that have to do with terminology. As described in a previous chapter, the term "ecology" means the study of living things and how they relate to one another and to their nonliving environment. If you say you are "protecting the ecology," what you really mean is that you are protecting your environment or ecosystem. Also, the correct pronunciation of ecosystem is with a long "e," not "echo-system," as it is sometimes pronounced.

It is not a coincidence that the countries with the best environmental protection policies are those that also have strong economies. It costs money to prevent pollution or to clean up after the fact, whether the costs are borne by the polluting industry or by the public. As already pointed out, a strong economy is by widely accepted definition a growing economy, therefore most people tend to see the positive relationship between environmental protection and economic growth. At the same time, there seems to be limited understanding that continuous economic growth is unsustainable in the long term and therefore its ultimate impact on the environment will be negative.

With increasing scale, the limitations of the environmental movement become more and more apparent. The larger the scale, the more difficult the challenges associated with maintaining a healthy environment. It is relatively easy to set aside some natural areas at the local or state level to preserve habitat for threatened species or to regulate waste discharges from an industry that has only local impact. On the other hand, it takes consensus and cooperation across state or national jurisdictions to protect the quality of air and water that knows no political boundaries, or to regulate the use of pesticides on food crops that may be shipped long distances.

Environmentalism tends to break down or at least be less effective at the global scale. For example, conversion of vast areas of tropical rain forest to row crops or pasture may be seen at the local or even national level as a beneficial and necessary practice. The forest provides lumber for a hungry global market and once the forest land is converted to crop land it can provide a decent living as well as food for many people for generations to come. On the other hand, destruction of many local or regional forests, when considered on a global scale, can have far-reaching environmental and economic consequences, including destruction of rare species habitat and eventual depletion of the world's sources of lumber. Thus the benefits may be primarily local and immediate but the true costs may be global and long-lived.

It is difficult for nations to work together on such transnational issues largely because of different perspectives. It is primarily the developed nations that are calling for forest preservation in undeveloped areas. However, most developed nations depleted their virgin forests long ago, which weakens their credibility with the developing nations that are converting their forests to what they consider more productive uses.

Global warming is perhaps today's most controversial global environmental issue and a good example of how the environmental movement lacks the clout needed to resolve biosphere-scale problems. I prefer to use the term "global warming" in this discussion instead of the more commonly used "climate change" because I believe that global warming is the best description of the problem while climate change is one of the predicted results of that problem.

To illustrate my point, I quote from a recent Associated Press article that referred to "ghost forests—dead trees along vast swaths of coastline invaded by rising seas, something scientists call one of the most visible markers of climate change." The fact that these trees are dying has nothing to do with climate change because their climate has not yet changed sufficiently to kill them. The trees are dying because of saltwater being pushed into what was formerly freshwater marsh as a result of rising sea levels. Rising sea levels are a direct result of melting ice and rising ocean temperatures—due to global warming.

I make the distinction not to deny climate change (as it is likely a major result that will need attention), but instead to focus on the apparent problem itself. Global warming is causing glacial ice to melt, which in turn is resulting in sea level rise. Global warming is a potential cause of climate change and other likely changes to the biosphere and is therefore the problem we should focus on.

Whichever term one prefers to use, the problem is both an environmental one and a political one. It's an environmental problem because it appears to be real and has potentially global scale environmental impacts. It is a political problem because many people refuse to believe it is real or contend that the steps necessary to halt it will have potentially devastating impacts on the established economic system. Also, there are those who believe that the whole idea that man could possibly have caused global warming is a hoax.

Let's deal with the hoax argument first. Glacial ice around the world, with perhaps a few local exceptions, has been steadily melting for more than a century. This is a well-documented fact that should not require any further debate. The prevailing scientifically credible theory for the cause of global warming is an increase in the "greenhouse effect" caused primarily by the gradual accumulation of carbon dioxide in the atmosphere as a result of mankind's burning of fossil fuels. This gradual increase in carbon dioxide is also well documented and the theory is supported by the fact that the increasing temperature of the earth correlates well with the increasing greenhouse effect.

If you believe global warming is a hoax, you have to ask yourself and be able to answer one essential question: what could cause glacial ice to melt on a global scale other than rising temperature on a global scale? When asked this question global warming skeptics typically respond with something like "well, maybe the warming is real, but it is caused by natural forces and is not caused by mankind's activities." Again, if this is your belief you need to be able to cite a theory that shows how and what natural forces could be causing the warming.

One such theory is that the relatively warm period of the twentieth and twenty-first centuries is a result of a natural increase in solar radiation compared to the several centuries of the Little Ice Age. While this theory may seem credible, the correlation of global temperature data with the intensity of solar radiation appears weak compared to the correlation with carbon dioxide levels as per the greenhouse gas theory. Regardless of the cause, global warming is likely to result in significant environmental and economic problems before there is strong enough consensus on the matter for the major producers of greenhouse gases to take meaningful action to reduce carbon dioxide production or find ways to remove it from the atmosphere.

Beginning in the late twentieth century, some reputable climatologists began predicting that there would soon be at least a few decades and perhaps a century or two of unusually cold climate that would be caused by a period of decreased solar output from the sun. This prediction was based on the fact that solar activity tends to cycle and that known periods of cold climate have occurred in the past, for example the so-called Little Ice Age which lasted several hundred years and ended around the dawn of the twentieth century. But even if a prediction of another Little Ice Age comes true, it does not invalidate the greenhouse gas accumulation theory; it may just mean that the full impacts of any man-caused global warming will be delayed.

Global warming and climate change are not subjects I wish to cover in any detail in this book; I use them merely to illustrate my premise that traditional environmentalism is by and large ineffective in dealing with issues of global concern. It is likewise ineffective in dealing with the premise of this book, which is that economic growth is not sustainable and may ultimately become the largest and most critical environmental issue ever faced by the human race.

CHAPTER 5

SUSTAINABILITY

I have used the word "sustainable" in previous chapters, but what does the term mean? One dictionary definition that is relevant to the subject of this book is "an action or process that is able to be maintained or kept going." Specifically, I wish to use the term to refer to maintaining an ecosystem and/or the earth's biosphere in a manner suitable for human habitation and not just for a few centuries, but basically forever, or at least until the next major asteroid impact.

The use of the term sustainable in the context of economics invariably leads to the subject of sustainable development or sustainable growth. Thanks to the United Nation's World Commission on Environment and Development (Brundtland Commission) we have a definition of sustainable development that has been widely adopted. The Commission's report, *Our Common Future* (1987) defines the term as "development that meets the needs of the present without compromising the ability of future generations to meet their own needs."

Development itself has many meanings depending on the context in which the term is used. For the purpose of this book, I prefer the definition put forth by Herman Daly (professor emeritus, University of Maryland), which I will paraphrase as actions taken to make a qualitative improvement in people's lives. The end result of qualitative improvement should be to raise the living standard of the overall population. In order to raise the average living standard of the overall population it would seem most important to adopt policies that provide more and better opportunities for those in most need.

When policymakers speak of development they are usually talking about economic development, which they generally consider as efforts to create jobs so as to improve living standards within their jurisdictions. As a practical matter, at least in the so-called developed nations, job creation generally results in population growth because new jobs are just as likely (or perhaps more so) to be filled by applicants living outside the target area, who may be more likely to have the needed skills, as to be filled by applicants already living in the area who may not have the needed skills or who may be less qualified than those wanting to move from outside the area. Thus economic development becomes synonymous with economic growth, often driven by population growth.

Another thing that policymakers in the United States do is compete with other jurisdictions for jobs by offering various incentives to attract industry. Such incentives range from tax breaks to providing water and sewer services and building roads, or even providing land at below market value. While such practices promote growth, they do not necessarily promote development in the sense of a qualitative improvement in people's lives. Beyond a certain point, such development generally results in higher taxes for the general public, higher rents, more regulations, greater traffic congestion, reduced air quality, and a general compromise of the free ecological services that nature provides. In the quest for growth, many amenities that are greatly desired in urban areas, such as sidewalks, bike paths, parks, and green space often get little attention.

Offering incentives to attract industry generally results in competition for growth among states. Even though our nation is known as the United States, this competition often results in division. If one state lures industry from another state the result is usually a winner and a loser economically. The governor of my state brags that his policies have helped make it the number one state in the nation for being business-friendly. Another way to put this might be that it is the number one state for corporate welfare. Such competition among states often results in bidding wars that essentially determine which state is willing to give up the most resources for the sake of growth—sometimes referred to as a race to the bottom—without thorough consideration of the net benefit or loss resulting from that growth.

Obviously there are other aspects of sustainability than just the economic and ecosystem issues. I believe that ethics should be a major consideration when evaluating whether a practice is sustainable. Luring industry from other areas by giving tax breaks and lowering environmental standards is an example of unethical practices because it has the potential of lowering living standards in both locales. Accumulating massive debt or depleting natural resources unethically transfers responsibilities to future generations that have no say in the matter today. Both geographic and generational ethics should be considered in the decision-making process used by any policymakers wishing to improve the economic condition of their constituents.

At what point does economic development become uneconomical? Clearly during the recent recession, many people saw the value of their homes decline as a result of the easy-money policies that led to speculative overbuilding. Builders and associated businesses went bankrupt or at least laid off employees, tax revenues declined, unemployment spiked, and the trickle down effects were felt by a large percentage of the population, especially among the least skilled workers who were often the first to lose their means of making a living. While many people believe the recession is over and good times are just around the corner, that view is hard for me to accept largely because of the huge amount of debt that has been amassed in both the public and private sectors.

Within the context of economic growth, is the notion of sustainable growth realistic? Can economic growth be sustained without compromising the quality of life of future generations? When one considers that economic growth depends on debt growth, resource depletion, and usually population growth, how can it be seen as sustainable over the long term? From an ecological standpoint, it clearly seems impossible. From a quality of life standpoint, it seems undesirable. I don't even understand how economists could defend the term "sustainable growth" as realistic.

I once attended a meeting sponsored by the local chamber of commerce at which a PhD rural sociologist from a major state university presented a talk about demographics, economic development, job skills, and so forth. He stated during the question and answer period that it was important for a community's economic health that it retain its young people and continue to recruit new people from outside the area. The time allotted for questions ran out before I had a chance to ask him whether such advice was applicable to all communities. I am sure he would have responded in the affirmative, and my follow-up question would have been "If every community is retaining its young where do the outsiders come from?" This is an example of how even highly educated people give little thought to sustainability.

The economic growth paradigm is so firmly entrenched in the psyche of policymakers that it can best be described as what psychologists refer to as "groupthink." This term refers to the desire for conformity and harmony within a group of people that is so strong that it results in irrational decisions. In such situations group members tend to refuse to consider alternative viewpoints and the result is suppression of individual thinking. I have frequently observed local government policymakers say something like "growth is going to come whether we like it or not, so we have to plan for it" while at the same time refusing to acknowledge that they are doing whatever they can to encourage growth.

A paradigm encompasses and reflects a pattern. It is a philosophical framework within which we view things. We do things this way because it has worked well in the past.

It's the way we have always done it! Our attitude about growth is one of today's most seriously entrenched paradigms. Our leaders cling to this growth equals progress paradigm steadfastly. It has become a sort of dogma, and as such it is very much like a religion.

I hesitate to mention religion but I believe it is relevant to the topic of this book. The *Merriam-Webster Dictionary* defines religion as "an organized system of beliefs, ceremonies and rules used to worship a god; or an interest, a belief, or an activity that is very important to a person or group." There are several well-known religions in the world and it is beyond the scope of this book to discuss them in any detail, but I believe that there is a very strongly entrenched religion that is not generally recognized as such at all, but fits the definition given above like a glove. The name of that religion is economic growth and its worshipers are many and very active throughout the world. Their bible says growth is always good and they are not about to question its authenticity.

It is a characteristic of the world's recognized religions that their most ardent believers often look down upon or even ostracize those among them who question their beliefs. Among the general population, at least in the developed world, anyone who questions the wisdom of perpetual economic growth is considered odd to say the least. Economic growth is indeed an organized system of entrenched beliefs and is held in such high esteem as to be worshiped much like a god is worshiped.

A former commission chairman of a nearby county once remarked at a public meeting that it was his belief that "if you are not growing you are dying." It would be hard to express the "grow or die" paradigm any clearer than that. While such a statement might be appropriate to use as a means of encouraging your child to take piano lessons seriously, it certainly makes no sense from the standpoint of sustainability. From an ecological perspective, if one species is growing in numbers it is likely that other species are shrinking in numbers or dying out entirely because their habitats are being destroyed. Ultimately the species that is growing in numbers will destroy its own habitat if that growth is taken to extreme. Perhaps sustainability could be seen as a compromise between "grow or die" and "grow and die."

Zoning ordinances are common ways for local governments to direct how and where development occurs. Typical zoning divides land into agricultural, residential and commercial uses. These broad categories may be further subdivided; for example residential areas may be allocated for single family or multi-family dwellings. Zoning can be a useful tool for local governments to develop reasonable plans for directing growth and development away from environmentally sensitive areas or simply to allow citizens some say in how land is used. Local governments, however, are generally forced into zoning and are usually quite receptive to changes whenever someone wants to revise the ordinance by rezoning a specific site to accommodate growth.

Progress is an often misused word in the context of sustainability. Progress is a term that is usually seen as good even when it is used to defend change in opposition to established plans in which the community has been involved in creating. For example, the city council where I live recently approved rezoning to allow demolishing a shopping area consisting of several small businesses in favor of developing a larger business, even before the actual name of the larger business was disclosed and in spite of considerable community opposition to the project. The rezoning resulted in a change to the so-called comprehensive plan for the city which the citizenry had some input into developing. Ironically, the city's planning board voted to recommend denial of the rezoning, with the lone dissenter on the board being quoted in the newspaper as voting for the rezoning because he did not want to be "against progress." It seems that no matter how much planning is done by local government the plans can easily be changed for the sake of growth or in the name of growth's corollary—"progress."

Progress implies a goal, but often the implied goal is simply growth, with no thought of whether it is needed, wanted, or sustainable. Should it not be obvious that the size of the economy cannot keep growing forever? Doesn't economic output ultimately depend on the resources the earth is able to provide in a sustainable way? Isn't the term "sustainable growth" an oxymoron? How can depletion of stored resources such as oil, natural gas, and water in subterranean aquifers be considered sustainable? In a world that is essentially out of frontiers, these are questions that need serious consideration, especially by policy makers. But with growth being worshiped like a god how likely is it that policy makers will consider such questions unless an overwhelming number of citizens begin asking them?

If we are to use the term *progress* when speaking of growth or development, then we need to think of it in terms of progressing toward a specific goal. Any development that does not create a better environment, especially for the neediest of society, should not be considered progress. All too often, so-called economic development results in such negative factors as greater congestion, more regulations, more air pollution, increased demand for scarce resources, and an overall decline in the quality of life in established neighborhoods, making it in reality uneconomic growth.

New technology that increases efficiency or makes more resources available is often cited as increasing sustainability. For example, the recently developed hydraulic fracturing technology (known as fracking) that allows vast amounts of oil and natural gas to be recovered from certain shale deposits has boosted production to the point where the United States has the potential of being a net exporter of those fuels. New technology has also allowed drilling in increasingly deeper ocean environments and in multiple directions from a single location.

Although new technology has made more fossil fuels available it does not change the fact that those fuels exist in a finite supply and their continued extraction is not sustainable over the long haul. Also, the increased cost of new technology may not be fully considered. Not only are the oil and gas recovery costs of fracking higher than conventional drilling, the collateral or unintended damage such as soil contamination from saltwater spills, ground subsidence (sinking at the surface as underlying cavities created by oil removal are filled in as gravity collapses the overlying rock and soil layers) and even earthquakes caused by the fracking process has not been fully assessed.

And how does new technology such as hydraulic fracturing that increases the supply of petroleum actually enhance sustainability? Granted, an increased supply of fuel will allow economic growth to be sustained for a longer period of time, but it will not likely be enough to last until the next major asteroid hits the earth. Sustainability is as misused a term as progress. Let's not think of something being sustainable if it only lasts a few centuries or less.

The local newspaper in my community recently reported that a newly discovered field of shale rock in west Texas could yield 20 billion barrels of oil plus 16 trillion cubic feet of natural gas. A professor at a Texas university was quoted in the article as saying it would take years before any significant amount of oil is recovered from this rock formation but he doesn't doubt the economic benefit that will follow. And here's the part that made my jaw drop: the professor was quoted as saying, "The revival of the Permian Basin is going to last a couple of decades." The largest source of shale oil the US Geological Survey has ever assessed and it is only going to last a couple of decades? Surely the professor was misquoted, but in any event it calls attention to the lack of understanding regarding the sustainability of stored energy.

Failure to fully assign costs is a common practice among economists and policymakers. It is common to allow private companies to pocket the profits from their businesses while ignoring the collateral costs that are eventually paid for by the public. Such things as damage to buildings caused by earthquakes or ground subsidence or pollution of groundwater are examples of costs that may be borne by people living considerable distance from hydraulic fracturing sites and who see no benefit from the oil or gas extraction. Perhaps if costs could be fully assessed it would call needed attention to the issue of sustainability.

CHAPTER 6

FUELING ECONOMIC GROWTH

Mankind first used stored energy way before the dawn of recorded history by burning wood to cook food, ward off nighttime chills and to generate light for working at night or inside caves (cave paintings in France have been radiocarbon dated to before 30,000 BC from torch marks on cave walls). Wood, while not a stored energy source in the same sense as fossil fuels, is indeed energy stored by trees as a result of photosynthesis. Although wood produces relatively little energy output compared to fossil fuels such as coal, petroleum or natural gas, it is a renewable energy source as long as forests are managed wisely.

Coal, probably the first fossil fuel to be exploited, could be found in many locations lying on the ground or in exposed seams along fault lines or in cliff faces. In different parts of the world, people independently discovered that this black "rock" could be used for fuel. Archeologists have found evidence of surface mining of coal and its use in households in China dating from around 3,500 BC. The Greek scientist Theophrastus wrote about coal being used for metalworking around 300 BC. The Romans were exploiting coal fields in Britain as early as the second century AD. In the western hemisphere the Aztecs were using coal for fuel and ornaments when the Spanish encountered them in the sixteenth century.

First wood and then coal were used extensively to power steam engines in various applications. The first practical steam engines, invented by Thomas Newcomen in 1712, were used primarily to pump water out of coal mines. Although the Newcomen engines were extremely inefficient they were widely used for over sixty years in much of Europe before James Watt (who is often credited with inventing the steam engine) figured out how to make vast improvements. Gradually steam engines evolved to the point where they were practical to power various kinds of machinery and eventually they were developed to the point that they could be used to power locomotives and boats. The efficient use of steam power launched the industrial revolution and with it the consumption of coal really took off.

Man has also used petroleum in various forms since ancient times. Tablets from ancient Persia indicate the use of petroleum for lighting and medicine by the upper classes of society. According to the Greek historian Herodotus, asphalt was used more than four thousand years ago for building walls and towers in Babylon. While we may think of asphalt as a man-made product, it was originally a naturally occurring viscous liquid or semi-solid form of petroleum. The well-known La Brae tar pits in California and the Athabasca tar sands in Canada are examples of natural asphalt deposits. The asphalt we use today to pave roads is produced as part of the petroleum refining process.

The general public began to recognize the value of petroleum only after the kerosene lamp became widely used in the mid-1800s and later when the automobile was invented in the late nineteenth century. The kerosene lamp began to replace whale oil lamps after the process to distill kerosene from petroleum was invented in 1847 by James Young in Derbyshire, England. Young set up a small business that refined crude oil in 1848 and in 1851 he and other partners established the first commercial oil refinery in Bathgate, Scotland. The refinery exploited local oil shale and coal deposits.

Once chemists began refining various products from petroleum it wasn't long before the internal combustion engine was developed. The first commercially successful one was produced in Paris by a Belgian expatriate named Jean Joseph Lenoir. Although Lenoir's engine was used to power a prototype three wheeled vehicle in 1863, most of his engines were used for stationary power to run such things as water pumps and printing presses. The Lenoir engines did not compress the fuel charge and therefore were low-horsepower and low-efficiency machines.

Nikolaus Otto was a young traveling salesman for a grocery company when he happened to see one of Lenoir's engines in Paris in 1860. Intrigued, Otto began experimenting with a replica of Lenoir's engines and soon began to realize that he could improve the engine's efficiency if he could design it to compress the fuel charge before it ignited. In 1876, after much trial and error, Otto and his associate Eugen Langen succeeded in producing the first internal combustion engine that compressed the fuel prior to ignition. This engine (which ran on an illuminating gas such as acetylene or natural gas) operated at far higher efficiency than any prior engine design.

With the invention of the carburetor and other improvements internal combustion engines were developed that ran on gasoline, which itself went through an evolutionary process of refinement and blending of additives before it became the fuel we know today. Diesel engines, which use no spark plugs but ignite fuel by compression only, were developed during the same period as gasoline engines and have several advantages over them, particularly for powering large vehicles such as trucks, trains, and buses.

Natural gas is a fossil fuel that was relatively late to be exploited on an industrial scale by humans. According to Wikipedia, gas seeping from the ground was used by the Chinese as early as 500 BC to boil seawater for extracting salt. Natural gas seeping from rocky outcrops in southwestern Turkey has allegedly been burning for nearly three thousand years and it is quite likely that these flames were exploited early by humans at least for cooking.

The first modern commercial production of natural gas began at Fredonia, NY, in 1825. In the 1880s, natural gas was most commonly encountered as a byproduct of producing liquid petroleum. Because of the cost of capturing and transporting this byproduct it was not economical to use it unless there was a ready market for it near the wellhead. As a result, in the nineteenth and early twentieth centuries, unwanted gas was burned off as it escaped from the oil wells. Today much of this so-called stranded gas is injected back into the oil reservoir to re-pressurize it to enhance oil production.

Natural gas is composed of hydrocarbons (mostly methane) and is formed from decomposing plant and animal matter under extreme heat and pressure. It is a cleaner burning fuel than either coal or petroleum. Today it is used extensively to power electric generating plants and to heat homes and businesses. It is also used to produce hydrogen, ammonia-based fertilizers and to run some vehicles. Like coal and petroleum, natural gas is considered non-renewable because it is thought to take millions of years to form yet only a very short time to consume.

The description of various fuels and engines in the above paragraphs is meant to illustrate not only how economic growth has been fueled, but also the concept of substitutability, which I mentioned earlier as an important concept of economics. But notice that the fuels mentioned above are essentially non-renewable, except for whale oil and wood, which produce relatively little energy. Whale oil is now essentially nonexistent due to past over-harvest of whales and a ban on whale harvest by most nations. Wood is still used to some extent for fuel but most woods are more valuable for other uses and over-harvest of wood is also a problem in many parts of the world.

Pound for pound, gasoline produces about five times (and coal about double) the heat output of wood. Production, distribution and storage costs, cleanliness, and many other factors combine to make coal, petroleum, and natural gas the fuels of choice for our modern economy.

However, these fossilized fuels were formed and stored in the earth over many millions of years and they are being consumed at rates that will likely deplete them in a few hundred years. Thus it should be obvious that the size of today's economy is largely a result of the use of stored energy that is not being renewed at a significant rate. It seems just as obvious that an economic system that depends on the consumption of ever-increasing amounts of such energy must be considered unsustainable.

How fast is the world consuming its oil supply? Something over 91 million barrels per day, according to a January 2015 Associated Press report. That's the equivalent of, on average, every human on the planet using a half gallon of oil every day. Remember, that is average use for the globe. A large percentage of the world's population uses very little oil, so per capita usage in the so-called developed countries is much higher than the average. The reader can imagine what the per capita usage would be if all nations were to achieve the same level of development as the more wealthy nations.

That same Associated Press report stated that geologists estimate the world's proven petroleum reserves stands at about 1.7 trillion barrels. It is worth repeating that 1.7 trillion barrels is what geologists estimate is known to be underground, but not what is technically or economically feasible to extract from the ground. Much of the known reserves cannot be extracted economically using today's technology.

Now, 1.7 trillion barrels sounds like a lot, but at today's consumption rate that is only enough to last a bit over fifty years. Not long, especially when you consider the fact that we have only been using petroleum since 1859, when the industry was born with the first successful oil well in Pennsylvania. Putting this all in perspective, the world's entire oil reserves could conceivably last less than 1 percent of the time that has elapsed since human beings first began recording history somewhere around 3,500 BC. Another way to put it is to say that the use of petroleum to fuel economic activity is just a quickly passing phenomenon in the context of human endeavors.

It is also worth noting that geologists continue to find likely new petroleum sources and over the last twenty-five years the reserve estimate has actually increased at a slightly faster rate than the world's consumption. In 1980 the proven reserve estimate was 683 million barrels; if that were all that was actually available at that time, the world would likely have run completely out of oil by now. If geologists keep finding new sources at the rate of the last twenty-five years, by the end of the current decade the reserve estimate may well be in the neighborhood of two trillion barrels. How much of that will be technically and economically available is anybody's guess. The more difficult it gets to identify new petroleum sources, the more likely it is that the cost of extraction will be so high as to make the product prohibitively expensive for the average consumer.

The recently introduced hydraulic fracturing system (fracking) for recovering petroleum has made it technically feasible to extract oil from sources previously considered too difficult to tap. But the economics of fracking depends on a relatively high price of oil; the breakeven price has recently been reported in the press as somewhere around $50/barrel. As a comparison, to help put $50/barrel oil into perspective, it is said that Saudi Arabia can profitably extract oil when the price is $15/barrel. The calculated economic cost of extraction of petroleum by fracking of course does not include the potential unintended and difficult to quantify costs that I have already mentioned. Obviously the relative cost of fracking compared to more traditional means of extraction will come down as the more easily obtainable oil reserves are depleted

There are also unintended environmental costs associated with natural gas recovery. According to a January 25, 2016, article in *Time Magazine* an estimated 100 billion cubic feet of natural gas each year leaks from storage facilities in the United States alone. A well-publicized leak at Alison Canyon in California, one of the nation's largest gas storage reservoirs, spewed an estimated sixty-five thousand pounds of methane gas per hour into the atmosphere. The leak was discovered in October 2015 and was not plugged until February 2016. An estimated ninety-five tons of methane and seven thousand tons of ethane leaked into the atmosphere before the leak was contained. Methane gas is considered a more powerful greenhouse gas than the carbon dioxide we hear so much about. The methane leaked each day from Alison Canyon is estimated to equal the daily greenhouse gas emissions of 4.5 million cars.

The relatively high cost of extracting much of America's petroleum reserves may be a good thing in the long run if it means the oil will be available over a longer period of time. Whether it lasts a half century or two centuries, the fact remains that oil will be depleted in a very short period of time relative to the length of time humans have had a significant impact on the earth. The use of oil and other fossil fuels has enabled humankind to achieve a population density and overall standard of living that cannot be maintained after the fuels are depleted unless other major and sustainable fuel sources are discovered.

Will there be a new safe and sustainable fuel developed before the world runs out of its fossil fuel supply? Some say fuel cells hold considerable promise for improving energy efficiency and reducing pollution. But fuel cells run on hydrogen, and hydrogen is produced by electricity or by processing coal or natural gas. In other words, the fuel to run fuel cells will come primarily from fossil fuels.

There is nuclear fission, which is now widely used in many nations. When fission power plants were first conceived the general public was promised electricity so cheap that there would be no need to meter it. Today, however, the cost to build a new plant, in the US at least, is astronomical. A nuclear project in Georgia, initially estimated to cost $14 billion is now projected to cost at least $25 billion, according to press reports. A similar project in South Carolina has recently been canceled because of cost projections nearly double the original estimate. In addition to the high cost to build new nuclear power plants, the immense problems associated with the storage and disposal of wastes, and the danger of serious accidents make nuclear fission an unlikely substitute for fossil fuels anytime soon.

Lockheed Martin Corporation announced in 2014 that it is developing a nuclear fusion reactor that will be compact enough to fit on the back of a large truck. The company acknowledges that many key challenges need to be overcome, but is optimistic that a working prototype can be developed in about five years (2020) and an initial production version in ten. The fusion reactor would run on hydrogen and the company claims the energy produced by fusion will be three to four times more powerful than that produced by fission. However, Lockheed is seeking help with this project, which would seem to indicate that it may not be as close to fruition as expected. And I would venture to guess that the cost will be quite high indeed.

As can be seen from the above discussion, the economic concept of substitutability as it relates to fuel supply has worked, at least so far. What if a practical nuclear fusion reactor is indeed on the horizon? Will the earth's fossil fuel supply last long enough for this new technology to replace existing power plants? And what about fuel to run cars and trucks? Can a fusion reactor be made small enough to power the vehicles we depend on every day?

Even though fossil fuels (coal, oil, and natural gas) are essentially non-renewable (because it took millions of years to produce them), the earth may still contain enough to last for a few hundred years, or perhaps more in the case of coal. There is no way to accurately estimate just how long these fuels will last; it's safe to assume that they haven't all been discovered yet, and we will likely get better at extracting those we have already found. If the rest of the world were to suddenly achieve the standard of living we enjoy in the United States, as supported by our fuel consumption, then a thousand years supply of fuel based on today's consumption rate would last only about a century.

This chapter would not be complete without some discussion of renewable energy sources other than wood (which I have already mentioned). The major renewable sources available today include hydroelectric, solar, wind and geothermal (all of which are not only renewable but are essentially emissions free). At present, all these sources combined are supplying only a small percentage of humanity's total power needs.

Hydroelectric power is generated by utilizing gravity to force water to flow through turbines. The most common form of hydropower is produced by building dams to create head pressure to turn the turbines. The deeper the water behind the dam the greater the pressure and the more electricity is produced from a given volume of water. Water has been used to power various mechanical devices since ancient times but the generation of electricity by water power began only after the electromagnetic generator was developed in the late nineteenth century. Today hydropower is widely used around the world, but it accounts for less than 20 percent of total electricity needs (less than 10 percent of needs in the United States). A big advantage of hydropower is that it can be brought online very quickly, basically by opening a valve. It is therefore very valuable for use when demand increases rapidly over a short time period.

While hydroelectric projects are still being built around the world (China's Three Gorges Project, completed in 2012 with a capacity of 22,500 megawatts, is the world's largest power station) in many countries (including the United States) there are few remaining practical sites to build new dams. Large hydropower projects displace many people and may destroy valuable ecosystems. Many valuable salmon and shad spawning runs have been disrupted by dams in the United States. China's Three Gorges project displaced over a million people from their homes and farms.

Solar power, generated directly by photovoltaics or indirectly by using mirrors or lenses to concentrate the heat from sunlight onto water tanks to produce steam to run conventional turbines, is a relatively new means of generating electricity. Solar power is a rapidly growing entity as technology matures and production costs drop. In 2014, the International Energy Agency predicted that solar would account for as much as 27 percent of the world's electricity needs by the year 2050 and that solar would by then be the world's largest single source of electricity.

Solar of course has its own drawbacks, the most obvious being that it only works well when the sun is shining. Solar works best in the world's mid-latitudes where days are longest. And if solar is going to provide electricity over a twenty-four-hour period there must be a way of storing energy to be released during the nighttime hours. Solar facilities also take up a lot of space and thus have the potential of disrupting wildlife habitat and destroying natural areas. But solar has considerable potential for small applications such as rooftops in underdeveloped countries where there is no electrical grid to connect to.

The mechanical power of wind has been utilized for many centuries to power ships and pump water. More recently, the power of wind has been harnessed to drive electrical generators. Large wind farms, both on land and offshore have been developed, and small wind generators for installation on rooftops or poles are also being produced. Wind power, or lack of it depending on the location, is generally consistent from year to year but varies a lot over days or weeks. It therefore works best where it can be connected to a grid where it can supplement other power sources. Denmark produces about 40 percent of its electricity from wind and on a worldwide basis wind supplies about 4 percent of electricity needs.

The first geothermal power station to produce commercial electricity was built in Italy in 1911 and was the only commercial producer until 1958 when a generating station was built in New Zealand. Today at least half a dozen nations produce 15 percent or more of their power needs with geothermal plants. Until recently geothermal plants have been restricted to areas where high temperature geothermal sources are near the surface of the earth. The newly developed binary cycle process can generate electricity at temperatures well below the boiling point of water and promises to expand the geographical range for practical geothermal applications.

There is little doubt that renewable energy sources will provide a greater portion of humanity's power needs in the future. They are already taking significant pressure off the demand for fossil fuels to supply those needs. However, I think it is unlikely that renewables will produce enough power to displace fossil fuels anytime in the foreseeable future. Most renewable sources cannot dependably supply continuous power, and thus the need for a stable grid to connect to—a grid fueled primarily by fossil fuels or nuclear reactors. Also, at present at least, it does not appear practical to power most of the world's vehicles solely by electric motors, natural gas or hydrogen.

To summarize the main point of this chapter let me emphasize that the world's economic growth has been the result of productivity gains fueled primarily by non-renewable energy sources. Most of these energy sources are rapidly being depleted and thus they cannot continue to support economic growth over the long term. While the economic concept of substitutability has worked sufficiently well so far to maintain increases in productivity, from an ecological perspective it does not appear to be a viable long term strategy.

CHAPTER 7

PROMOTING GROWTH

As I have already pointed out, economic success is measured in gross terms (gross domestic product or GDP). A constantly expanding economy is considered healthy, but any slow-down in the rate of GDP growth is seen as economic weakness. In this chapter, I will discuss some of the ways that economic growth is promoted and mention some of the pitfalls associated with growth. In addition to the manipulations of fiat money and credit by the Federal Reserve, five basic strategies are used by various levels of government and private business interests to promote economic growth, and thus a "healthy" economy. These strategies are population growth, productivity growth, depletion of finite natural resources, ever-increasing debt, and land use conversion.

In addition to the already discussed stimulus produced by the burning of fossil fuels, economic growth is constantly being encouraged in many other ways. Perhaps most serious is the widespread attempt to relentlessly encourage an increase in human populations by businesses, the press and by various levels of government. Population growth is a major component of economic growth because it generally contributes in a positive way to GDP growth. More people in any given area means that more products and services are produced, assuming of course that the newcomers are gainfully employed, and they don't take jobs away from those already living in the area.

Population growth is encouraged by most states and communities as a way to increase economic activity. Recall what I said earlier that GDP is a function of the total number of workers and their productivity. Thus if the number of workers is increased and other factors remain the same, GDP is increased. In the United States, our economic system developed over a period of time when there were plenty of new frontiers available for population expansion into relatively unsettled areas. Advances in technology, especially in the healthcare and food production and distribution fields, have facilitated population growth to the point that physical frontiers have little meaning in today's world. Does this mean that there are no longer any practical limits to growth, or will there be technology limits or perhaps unintended consequences of technology that will ensure that population growth does indeed have limits?

Some may argue that most communities don't overtly promote population growth but instead promote industrial or business growth and population growth is simply a byproduct. But why try to attract new industry or business into an area that already has a broad based economy except for the purpose of attracting more people? And it is clear that many communities do indeed overtly promote population growth. Recall the publication of the small town that I referenced in the introduction to this book. It billed the town as "as a place for new residents to find a welcoming home" and cited the chamber of commerce as working tirelessly to promote the town "as a place to live and work." The official local government website of the county where I live includes a promotional video that is clearly designed to attract new residents.

Those who hold the economy supreme ignore the possibility that there could ever be too many humans. Yet the world is full of examples of degraded human habitat barely supporting even a minimal living standard. Even in our so-called "land of plenty" we are constantly asked to lower our living standard (use fewer resources, tolerate more pollution and congestion and take on more debt) in order to accommodate more people in the name of economic growth. We spend precious resources to attract more people without any public discussion of what an optimum or sustainable population might be.

Elected officials go to great lengths to lure new industries to their states and communities and politicians who run against incumbents frequently argue that they would do a better job of "growing the economy" than the incumbent. States often compete for population to fuel their economies, even at the expense of their natural capital. Attracting major industry creates a surplus of jobs, which will in turn attract many new people to the state, generating more income and more tax revenues; all widely applauded as beneficial gross dollars for the economy, with no discussion and apparently no thought of whether there is indeed any net benefit, economic or otherwise, or what the net impact that additional people and infrastructure will have on the natural resources that sustain the economy and quality of life.

The Federal Aid Highway act of 1962 required all federally assisted projects in urban areas with greater than fifty thousand population to be part of a continuing comprehensive and cooperative planning process. The Fixing America's Surface Transportation Act of 2015 requires the planning process to address eleven planning factors, the first of which is to support the economic vitality of the metropolitan area. As a result of the 2000 census, several local jurisdictions in the county where I live were able to join together to meet the fifty thousand population goal, and thus the local metropolitan planning organization (MPO) was born. This MPO was then eligible to receive federal grant money (three "free" federal dollars for every local dollar spent) to use in the transportation planning process which amounts to another way of promoting economic development, i.e., growth.

I recently sat in on a meeting of the citizens advisory committee of the local MPO. During this meeting, an update on a regional freight study was presented. One of the main goals of this study is to reduce congestion and bottlenecks on the area's truck route system. A concurrent goal is to strengthen regional economic competitiveness by promoting economic development, including retaining major industries, and attracting new ones. In other words, the freight study appears to be designed to reduce congestion on the transportation system so that new growth can attract more trucks so that the system can stay congested.

I mentioned in a previous chapter that the current governor of Georgia has bragged about making the state the number one place in the nation for businesses to locate. This has been done by giving tax breaks, purchasing land for businesses to locate on, dedicating tax-supported construction funds for new roads and highway interchanges, and offering other incentives that deplete the public treasury. Much of the wheeling and dealing is done in secret so the public has little say in the process and is largely unaware of what is taking place until it is a "done deal."

Eben Fodor, in his book *Better not Bigger* describes what he calls the Urban Growth Machine, a coalition of well-funded and politically powerful individuals who have the potential to directly or indirectly benefit from population growth. The growth machine described by Fodor is powered mainly by wealth created by land speculation and real estate development. Major business interests supporting the growth machine include bankers, real estate developers, real estate attorneys, construction companies, building supply companies, and landowners. Many of these business interests are supported by local and regional organizations such as the Chambers of Commerce and Homebuilders Associations, for example—organizations that often promote a stronger pro-growth agenda than the individual members they represent. Made up of some of the most influential people in a community, the growth machine presents a formidable obstacle to anyone questioning its agenda.

The urban growth machine recognizes the importance of local government in promoting growth and uses its wealth and influence to support pro-growth politicians running for office. The machine recognizes that local government affects the degree to which land development can be profitable by manipulating land use zoning, regulations and fees. Local governments also have the power to divert public resources to build new roads, sewers and other infrastructure to support land development and can promote new development with tax incentives and subsidies. The growth machine's stranglehold on local governments effectively prevents them from considering the negative impacts of an ever-increasing population, thus there is no attempt made to determine whether the increase in numbers is good or bad for the community.

The news media are firmly on board with the promotion of economic, and therefore population, growth. A recent headline on the front page of the *Atlanta Journal/ Constitution* newspaper is a good illustration of this point. The headline read: "Honeywell News is Another Big Win for Georgia" and the article went on to speculate that the Honeywell project will involve a technology or software development center that is expected to create several hundred high-paying jobs. The "big win" headline amounts to an editorial opinion that the news is good for Georgia and at the same time implies a "loss" for some other state. This is certainly a good example of media bias and the mixing of news and editorial opinion.

The article cited above also mentions several other companies that have recently announced plans to locate or expand significant new technology operations in the metro Atlanta area. The article does not mention any possible downside to or even mention the population growth that will occur as a result of these job creations. It's a safe bet that the population will increase with the job creations because these jobs will be filled primarily by people moving in from other states. After all, Georgia doesn't have that many unemployed technology-savvy residents looking for work; such individuals are most likely already gainfully employed.

Ironically, in the same edition of the Atlanta paper, was an article reporting that the city of Atlanta had received a $5.6 million federal grant that will allow the city to hire nearly fifty new firefighters. The grant money is coming from the Department of Homeland Security and the Federal Emergency Management Agency. It seems to me that the irony is that the addition of so many people to the city's population is seen as such a benefit even while the city has to rely on outside grant money to upgrade its fire department. If growth is such a good thing, why can't growth pay for the new firefighters instead of having to depend on a federal government grant to fund them?

The news and entertainment industries support growth for obvious reasons. A growing population results in more people to buy newspapers, listen to radio, watch television shows or use the internet. A wider audience for news and entertainment outlets means more advertising and the additional advertising can be sold at a higher price because it reaches more people.

Other retail business owners support population growth for the same reasons the news and entertainment industries do. More people equates to increased sales. The same with manufacturers; more people mean more products to sell. But I have often wondered how many small businesses really benefit from growth or if growth eventually increases competition from large retailers that can undercut small businesses in price and put them out of business. Indeed the downtown business districts in many small towns have been destroyed by competition from large retailers. Nevertheless, small businesses seem to support efforts to lure new industries and people as much as larger firms do. Small businesses seem to support chambers of commerce as readily as larger ones. Perhaps the typical small business owner hopes that a growing population will be the catalyst that turns hers into a large business.

Our nation grew strong because of vast open spaces for population expansion, abundant natural resources, and a political system that rewarded individual efforts to become successful. Resource exploitation led to economic strength, a strong economy attracted a growing population, a growing population escalated resource demands, and so on. No wonder population growth and economic growth became synonymous, but how can such a "frontier economy" continue to function as frontiers disappear? Common sense tells us that our growth-dependent economic system is unsustainable and demands a serious search for a viable alternative.

Is the smart growth concept that has gotten considerable publicity in recent years the answer? The concept takes many forms, but a common goal is to reduce sprawl by concentrating new residential construction near jobs and leaving more undeveloped land in some semblance of its natural state. These seem like laudable goals, but is smart growth any better than dumb growth if the long-term result of both is a population so dense as to destroy the very resource base that sustains us all? In a previous chapter I compared growth to a religion and I believe that is a fair analogy. Another way of describing it would be as an obsession—and from an ecological perspective, a dangerous obsession at that!

Most people go about their lives as if they consider the ecosystem a part of our economy and believe that if we spend some money to control pollution, use our recycle bins, and clean up wastes, all will be well. In reality, precisely the opposite is true; our economy is part of the ecosystem and ecosystems are subject to limitations. If we grow our economy beyond the ecosystem's ability to support it, we must ultimately face the consequences. In the long run, the ecosystem will prove far more resilient than the economy, but we may not like how nature resolves the inherent conflicts between the two.

From an ecological standpoint, population density of any species is significant. A species that expands beyond the capacity of its habitat ultimately degrades that habitat and suffers consequences. People who raise animals for a living must be careful to maintain herds within the carrying capacity of their fields or their land will be degraded. Wildlife managers closely monitor deer populations and set hunting regulations with both sustainable habitat and sustainable harvest in mind, striving for what they consider an optimum population density. There is no reason to expect that human populations are not subject to the same principles of carrying capacity.

In addition to population growth, growth of debt is probably the most important driver of economic growth at least in the United States if not the world over. Debt proliferation has become so rampant as to become the very foundation of our economy. In less than half a lifetime the United States has gone from the world's largest creditor nation to the largest debtor. Corporate, private, and government debt are all at or near unprecedented levels. Such rampant increase in debt has helped fuel growth by shifting the cost of growth largely to future generations.

To Adam Smith, the eighteenth-century Scottish philosopher I have already mentioned and regarded by many as the founder of modern economics, acquiring and keeping capital (wealth) was as much a moral issue as an economic one. Smith stressed the importance of industrious behavior, saving for the future, and leaving future generations better off than one's own. Smith believed that this was the way that individuals, and nations, bettered themselves. I tend to agree with Smith on these issues, and I can't help but wonder how he would view the philosophies of today's economists.

The modern version of capitalism as practiced by the United States has abandoned the whole idea of building wealth for future generations in favor of requiring future generations to pay for today's largess. We frequently hear that our economy is driven by consumption, but since much of today's consumption is fueled by ever-increasing debt it seems clear that debt forms the very basis of our economy. Everywhere we turn, we are urged to borrow more money to live beyond our means so that economic growth will continue unabated. This debt-fueled growth is certainly unsustainable. Debt must be repaid in some manner, either by paying back the principle with interest or by suffering the consequences of default.

In 1946, public debt (our national debt) stood at approximately 122 percent of GDP as a result of the expense of World War II. This debt then gradually declined over the years, to about 33 percent of GDP in 1981. During the 1980s the national debt tripled. As a percentage of GDP, debt rose steadily from 1982 until the mid-1990s to about 65 percent of GDP. From 1996 until 2001 the debt declined somewhat as a percentage of GDP, but since 2001 it has increased rapidly and stands at approximately 105 percent of GDP (February 2016). At present the national debt stands at nearly $20 trillion and state and local debt amount to an additional $3.1 trillion in round figures. Thus total state, local and national public debt amounts to about $68,000 for each citizen of the United States. And yet it is still common to hear prominent citizens refer to the US as the world's richest nation. Surely those who make such statements have given the subject of debt little thought.

Personal debt has also risen substantially, now amounting to over $17 trillion. The main component of personal debt is mortgage debt, which amounts to nearly $14 trillion. Student loan debt ($1.3 trillion) and credit card debt ($942 billion) make up most of the remainder. Total personal debt adds up to about $54,000 for each individual citizen. Total US debt, which includes federal, state, and local government debt, household debt, business debt, and financial institution debt roughly amounts to a whopping $65 trillion. Adam Smith would surely be flabbergasted!

Considering the rapid increase in government, corporate and private debt over the past few decades it seems obvious that the recent stock market bubble was financed by debt. In other words, the public borrowed money at unprecedented levels to gamble on the stock market, while growing government deficits and corporate borrowing helped create an impression of good times.

Productivity is an important factor in economic growth. Recall that gross domestic product is a function of the number of workers and their productivity. Thus, if the number of workers is increased through population growth and their productivity is increased by the more efficient use of machinery or other technology then GDP increases in two ways. However, productivity is generally increased by exploiting more fossil fuels or other natural resources such as rare earth elements and water. I have already devoted a chapter to the unsustainable use of fossil fuels so there is no need to repeat myself. Just understand that whether we talk about steam engines or personal computers, technology has historically depended on exploitation of finite natural resources.

There is one more common growth engine that, although theoretically sustainable, should not be considered so because of its many unintended consequences and high costs when taken to extreme. I am talking about land use conversion, changing how land is used (for example, turning farm or forest land into shopping malls or residential housing). Now, some may argue that land use conversion is simply driven by the other four growth engines and is therefore not an engine in its own right. However, land is often converted to a different use specifically to attract growth, and such development does indeed fuel growth. Likewise, zoning is frequently changed to accommodate land use changes, which generally leads to more growth.

I said that land use conversion is theoretically sustainable. Farmland may become a residential neighborhood, which in turn might be razed and a factory built there, and it is possible that the factory could fall on hard times and the site could be returned to farmland. In such an unlikely scenario, land use could be converted indefinitely as long as food production and other ecological services could be maintained at sufficient levels. Typically, however, development is one way, toward a so-called "higher and better use" that earns the landowner (and government) increasingly higher income, but that need not always be the case.

According to the 2010 National Resources Inventory, a project of the Natural Resources Conservation Service, about 7.6 percent of the nation's total non-federally owned land area (excluding Alaska) was considered developed (built up areas and transportation routes), and average development nationwide was proceeding at about 0.1 percent of total land area per year. About 23 percent (316 million acres) of nonfederal rural land is considered prime farmland. About 13 million acres of this prime farmland has been lost, primarily to development, since 1982.

Some people cite the small proportion of developed land as evidence that man has little impact on the earth and argue that development can go on a long time without significant ecosystem effects. But mankind's impact reaches far beyond developed land; the amount of biologically productive land required to provide everything he uses (ecological footprint) includes virtually every major ecosystem, from the most remote jungles to the vast ocean depths. When that ecological footprint is fully considered, it should be clear that land use conversion as we know it today is ultimately unsustainable.

Let's take a closer look at mankind's ecological footprint. Humans have directly transformed more than half of the earth's approximately 50 million square miles of ice-free land (Hooke, et al.). This transformed land has been converted to cropland, pasture, cities, transportation networks, reservoirs, quarries, etc. About 40 percent of the remaining land is either desert, tundra, or high mountains that are largely off limits to significant human meddling. Much of the remaining land is forestland, but not necessarily virgin forest.

Based on the above figures one can readily see that man's total ecological footprint covers about three-fourths of the earth's land area and virtually all the oceans, which are being exploited at unsustainable levels, as I will mention in a later chapter. Bear in mind that this footprint is mostly a result of the high living standard of developed nations. The earth simply does not have the capacity to support all peoples of the earth at a living standard comparable to that seen in the more wealthy nations.

The unintended consequences of changing land use are many. Soil erosion is an obvious consequence that I dealt with often throughout my career as a fisheries biologist. I saw fish spawning areas and aquatic insect habitat choked with sediment and the overall productivity of many streams greatly diminished. I saw ponds and lakes reduced in depth and area because of sediment. By far the most severe and wide ranging erosion problems resulted from the lack of effective measures to retain sediment on sites where land was being graded for development.

Other common ecological effects of land use conversion include increased stream flows during wet times and reduced flows during droughts, both due to the increase in hard surfaces which invariably come with development. Many people who have had dependable wells for years have seen them go dry because of increased demand on receding water tables brought about by the increased demands of new homes or industry.

Folks who live near streams become afraid for their children to play in them because of the increasing levels of mud and trash and foam as the watersheds get built up. I have already mentioned the US Geological Survey study published in 1995 that revealed that urban streams in the Atlanta area supported about half the number of fish and a little over half the number of native fish species compared to a mostly forested watershed southwest of Atlanta. Such impacts on wildlife are a direct result of land use changes in the watersheds.

There are also many social changes associated with land use conversion. These may be good or bad, depending on one's point of view, and also depending on how much and how fast conversion takes place. From an ecological standpoint, one would expect a positive benefit/cost ratio associated with development up to some optimum population density, and then a negative ratio as density continued to increase beyond optimum. The higher taxes often seen in the most densely populated areas tend to support this reasoning.

So it seems clear that population growth is promoted by a huge segment of the public and is maintained in a variety of ways. In the next chapter I will explore some of the costs associated with growth that are often ignored.

CHAPTER 8

THE COST OF GROWTH

Growth comes with a price tag, but the numbers on that tag are often obscured by the rhetoric associated with the grow-or-die paradigm that constantly touts the alleged benefits of more growth. In this chapter I want to bring to light some of the information that can be found on growth's price tag if one is willing to look. Revealing specific dollar amounts for the cost of growth is difficult, but then the specific dollar amounts of the benefits are nearly always hard to pin down as well. The costs of growth can be grouped into three general categories: economic, social, and environmental.

A number of studies have documented the economic costs of growth and I refer the reader again to Eben Fodor's *Better not Bigger* for further reading on that subject. Some of the economic costs include increased debt (municipal and school bonds are examples of local debt), increased cost of maintaining infrastructure, and the cost of new roads and bridges needed to handle increased traffic. The cost of new roads and bridges increases tremendously with increasing population density because of the increased expense of acquiring rights of way, demolishing existing buildings and relocating utilities in more densely developed areas. The bottom line will be higher taxes for all to pay to cover the costs of these needs.

It is common for the pro-growth crowd to argue that attracting new industry (and more people) will expand the tax base and lead to lower taxes for homeowners since business property typically is assessed at a higher value than residential. This may be true for sparsely populated areas but as population density continues to increase everyone has to pay higher taxes to pay for the costs of the growth that goes beyond optimum density. Millage rates may stay about the same, but property values will increase with increasing population density, thus the net tax will increase for the average property owner. For those who don't own real estate the property tax increases will be passed on in higher rental rates.

The claim that industry helps shift the tax burden away from residential taxpayers is widely used as a reason to spend public money to lure new businesses. But that argument falls flat on its face when one considers all the money spent to lure new industry and subsidize it with tax breaks and other incentives, much of which residential taxpayers are on the hook for.

Another frequently proffered excuse for promoting growth goes something like this: "growth is going to come whether we want it or not, so we have to plan for it." This argument also fails the test of common sense. If growth is going to happen anyway, why spend so much money deliberately trying to attract it? It would be much easier and less expensive to plan for growth that "just happens" than to plan for and pay for the additional growth that is deliberately sought.

Not so obvious costs of growth include the backlog of infrastructure and facility maintenance needs that tend to get shoved onto the back burner as officials tend to delay such costs in order to pay for the needs of new development while trying to avoid raising property taxes. The city where I live recently proposed adding a tax based on the area of impervious surfaces on a property in order to pay for upgrading storm water management infrastructure that is gradually becoming obsolete. Interestingly enough, there has been a rather vocal outcry against the proposal, primarily from the same perpetual growth supporters who have advocated the government policies that have led to the problem.

I mentioned in a previous chapter that the city of Atlanta had received a federal grant that will allow for the hiring of new firefighters. My local community uses grant money to fund public transportation that can't come close to paying for itself with rider fees. Such grant money from the federal or state government typically comes with little cost to the local grantee, so it may not be perceived by the local community as a cost of growth. But grant money is not free; someone (people paying taxes) has to pay for it. Federal and state grants have often become a means of disguising the true cost of growth to local communities. Of course, anything that disguises the cost of growth makes it easier for the urban growth machine to perpetuate the myth that more growth is always good.

Some studies have concluded that economic growth increases income inequality and that income inequality in turn is a drag on economic growth. This makes sense when you think about it. One of the drivers of economic growth is productivity which increases as machines take over more and more tasks traditionally performed by human hands. This results in more people without jobs and more people competing for lower paying jobs while those who have the skills to operate the machines can generally expect a higher wage. As increasing numbers of people find themselves out of work or not making a living wage they turn to social services or charity to survive. These increased demands for social services then act as a drag on the economy because of the decreased productivity of those needing the services.

A September 2017 Federal Reserve Bulletin reported that both wealth and income inequality are getting worse. In 2016 the richest 1% of families in the United States controlled 38.6% of the nation's wealth and brought in 23.8% of income. The bottom 90% of families held just 22.8% of the wealth and earned less than half of the nation's income (49.7%). By contrast, the bottom 90% of families controlled about one third of the wealth in 1989 when the Fed began recording this measure. During that same period from 1989 to 2016 economic growth as measured by GDP nearly doubled from just under nine trillion to nearly 17 trillion dollars. These data seem to clearly demonstrate that growth in GDP is beneficial to those who are already wealthy but it also helps rob the poor of what little wealth they have.

The social costs of growth are often directly related to local officials' efforts to hold the line on property taxes that would otherwise have to be increased in order to maintain services citizens have come to expect. Such services include essential police and fire protection, but also things like public libraries, community centers, parks and recreational facilities and maintaining infrastructure. Logically, one would think that funding for such services should increase with the increased demands of a larger population. However, officials are often more likely to fund programs and policies that continue efforts to promote and entice more growth than they are to concede that growth has failed to generate the money needed to maintain the public services that many people have come to depend on. My local government recently reduced library hours and closed a branch library in order to avoid raising taxes to generate the money necessary to maintain the level of service that citizens had come to expect.

The general public is quite adverse to any tax increases, and this is understandable because the more one pays in taxes the less one has for spending on other things that seem more tangible. Many politicians continue to deny the need for tax increases, claiming instead that budgets can be balanced by ending wasteful spending. But I am aware of no proposals by either political party that specifically identify enough wasteful spending to eliminate that would balance the budget without raising taxes. Many politicians also continue to advocate more growth as a means of producing additional revenue to balance the budget. They do not seem to realize (or they are not willing to admit) that the increased growth simply puts more demand on services than is generated in revenue.

In a stable community where population is not increasing, taxes tend to also be stable from year to year because the primary need is to pay for operation and maintenance of existing facilities and for salaries of a steady workforce of public employees. Contrast this with a growing community where not only are taxes required to pay for operation and maintenance of existing infrastructure and salaries of existing employees but they must also pay for the cost of new roads, bridges, traffic lights, fire stations, schools, and of course, the salaries of new employees. Such additional costs are not borne solely by new residents. On the contrary, the costs are spread among the entire population so everyone's taxes must increase to pay for these increased costs.

Taxes are somewhat of an intangible expense in that when one pays a tax bill one does not get a tangible item in return, unlike when one buys a new television set or refrigerator, for example. Instead, taxes go into a government controlled fund that is then used to pay for things that the average person may not notice or if he does notice he may not associate it with the check written months ago to pay the tax bill. Thus, it becomes easier for the average person to resent tax increases because it is more difficult to understand the need or to even notice where the money goes. Politicians whose main goal is to get elected or reelected exploit this resentment by promising to hold the line on taxes.

Environmental costs associated with growth-related projects are typically ignored by economists. This is partly because environmental costs often come to light well after the projects are completed and the profits made, but also because environmental costs are usually hard to calculate, particularly in dollar terms. Environmental costs can be direct such as sedimentation of streams and lakes, but they can also be indirect as is the case with gradual declines in air or water quality, habitat loss, or introduction of non-native species.

Environmental costs of growth-driven activity are typically born by the public, whereas profits are usually realized by private individuals or corporations. Costs to the public can include direct damage to property or decline in property values due to proximity of undesirable industry or business. But public costs can also include declining air or water quality and/or increasing taxes that enable governments to enact and enforce regulations that minimize pollution.

The spread of exotic invasive species is an often unaccounted for cost to the public. As ocean-going cargo ships have increased in size and speed, the chances of hitchhiking aquatic organisms surviving on ships' hulls as they travel from port to port increases. Bilge water pumped in and out of ships loading and unloading provides another haven for hitchhiking species from foreign lands.

The zebra mussel (*Dreissena polymorpha*) is a good example of an unintentionally imported species that is wreaking havoc in many US waters. These small freshwater mussels are native to lakes in southern Russia and the Ukraine, but they have spread to North America and to many European countries where they have few natural predators to keep their numbers in check. In the United States, they first appeared in the great Lakes in the late 1980s and have since spread to the Mississippi River and most of its major tributaries as well as the St. Lawrence River. In addition to disrupting native ecosystems, the mussels have attached themselves to the insides of water intake pipes, causing major problems for municipal and industrial water suppliers.

Perhaps a better example for people living in the southern United States is the red imported fire ant (*Solenopsis invicta*). The fire ant is native to South America, but it has been accidentally introduced into the United States and a number of other countries, probably by way of shipping containers. Not only do these ants cause painful bites but they also contribute to millions of dollars in annual damage to livestock and agricultural crops.

The costs of growth are real, though not always apparent except in retrospect. Calculating the cost of growth up front is a bit like estimating the cost of going to war. The cost of fielding an army and providing it with supplies and materials for a given period of time is relatively easy for military logistics experts to estimate, but wars often last a lot longer or require more troops than initially planned, outcomes are uncertain, and there are often long term unforeseen consequences such as the costs of caring for or compensating disabled veterans. The Vietnam and Iraqi wars are both good examples. The environmental costs are often similar—unplanned, long term, and painful.

CHAPTER 9

EXPECTATIONS VS. REALITIES

Residents of the United States, and to some extent much of the western world's population, have come to expect many things as a result of continuous economic growth. In general, these expectations are for more and better things that constantly improve living standards. We have come to expect that each generation will be better off than the preceding one. In the US, such expectations are often referred to as having something to do with the "American dream." Though not relevant to this book, I think it somewhat odd how we in the United States have co-opted the term "American" as if the citizens of all those other nations to the north and south of us are not also Americans. In this chapter, let's look at some of those lofty expectations and contrast them with the realities that one might see if viewed from an ecological or even a common sense perspective.

We expect our standard of living to constantly rise from generation to generation; that is to say we expect each generation to be better off financially, live in bigger and better homes and have more material goods to make our lives better than that of the previous generation. After all, if we expect GDP to constantly rise, should we not expect that that increased production would benefit us all? The reality is that GDP does not constantly rise, recessions, and depressions happen. Our strong dependence on debt to finance our living standard has helped prolong the "American dream" myth but at the same time it guarantees that some future generation(s) will have to pay the bills we pass on to them, maybe even turning the dream into a nightmare. The steady drain on finite natural resources also guarantees that these resources will ultimately be unable to support higher living standards.

We expect to find steady employment that pays a living wage, and we expect to receive regular pay raises that will enable us to steadily improve our standard of living. Unless we have special skills or the right connections, however, the reality is that the same technology that increases the efficiency of production is steadily eliminating jobs that we took for granted as recently as a decade ago. Anyone who needs the income from a job in order to make a living is finding it increasingly difficult to compete with robots that are able to perform similar tasks. Once a robot is installed and operating it is basically slave labor, no need to pay it wages or benefits and it can work around the clock without violating any labor laws.

We expect a growing economy to improve living conditions for everyone, but the reality is that as the economy grows in size the wealthy are getting wealthier and the poor are getting poorer. As populations increase there is greater competition for resources. As we come to depend more and more on technology in the manufacturing and service industries those with the least skills face greater competition for the lowest paying jobs. Expanding global trade increases worldwide competition and puts further downward pressure on wages.

Many people living in the United States believe it is the world's richest nation, and I frequently hear it referred to as such by prominent citizens. In reality, though, how can it be the world's richest nation when government and personal debt combined amounts to an average of over $120,000 per citizen? The reality is that the United States is far from the world's richest nation. Perhaps at one time it was, but now wealth is an illusion supported only by the willingness of other nations and wealthy individuals to buy our debt.

We expect to live longer than the generation before us. So far, advances in healthcare and better nutrition have allowed that to happen, at least on average. Global mean life expectancy, now close to seventy years, has more than doubled since the beginning of the twentieth century. In the United States, average life expectancy at birth was nearly seventy-nine years in 2010.

Life expectancy is closely related to income, up to a point. The Preston Curve, named for Samuel Preston who first described it, illustrates the relationship between life expectancy and per capita income. As one might expect, the Preston curve demonstrates that individuals born in poor countries cannot expect to live as long as those in rich countries. However, the link between life expectancy and income flattens out at high-income levels. In other words, at low income levels further income gains have a much more positive effect on life expectancy than additional income gains when incomes are already high.

Living longer comes at a cost. As people age their bodies tend to break down, just as they have in generations past. What is different today is that there are more and better treatment options for either curing or at least managing many of the diseases and infirmities commonly associated with old age. Those cures and treatments are expensive, however, and the reality is that someone has to pay the bills. In the US, once we reach age sixty-five, we expect Medicare to pay for most of the cost. But the longer we live, the greater the expense, and the reality is that not near enough money is going into Medicare to fund the program indefinitely. Reality also dictates that if we are going to live longer we must work longer to pay for treating the problems we will likely encounter in old age.

Another reality is that not everyone can afford health insurance. Thus the expectation of living long enough to be eligible for Medicare may not be realistic for many poor people. Medicaid may also be an expectation for the poor that conflicts with reality, because just like any government program, someone has to pay for it. The reality is that neither Medicare nor Medicaid is sustainable without increased funding as life expectancies continue to rise.

In the developed world we have come to take good healthcare for granted. We expect doctors to cure many of our common ailments by simply prescribing an antibiotic. The reality is that antibiotics have been overprescribed and the bacteria they target have been evolving to resist one antibiotic after another. It has been less than a hundred years since the British bacteriologist Alexander Fleming discovered the germ-killing qualities of an errant penicillin mold growing in one of his experimental cultures. It took the combined efforts of science, industry and government to convert this mold into a mass-produced medicine in time for use in World War II. Since then, over a hundred other antibiotic compounds have been introduced, but no new class of these drugs has been developed since the current century began. When you consider the number of people taking antibiotics plus the number of livestock that routinely get antibiotics in their feed, there are plenty of opportunities for drug resistant bacteria strains to develop.

The World Health Organization has warned that gonorrhea may soon become untreatable because of growing resistance to antibiotics. The same organization has also noted that a drug resistant form of tuberculosis is circulating in one hundred countries. Along with bacteria resistance to drugs comes increased risk associated with surgeries of any kind as bacteria can gain access to a surgical opening by way of any breech in the sterilization protocol. This means that even elective surgeries such as knee and hip replacements become increasingly risky because of the danger of infection by drug-resistant bacteria.

Ironically, the failure to develop new antibiotics fast enough to keep up with drug resistant germs may be at least partly due to economic restraints. In many cases, the cost of developing new antibiotics is likely to fall far short of the economic return to the drug company producing it.

Unlike drugs to control cholesterol or high blood pressure, which many people take on a daily basis, there is a much more limited market for antibiotics which are typically prescribed for short term use for a much smaller number of patients. Thus the reality is that the healthcare system we have come to take for granted may not be as secure as we have come to expect.

We expect to achieve health insurance coverage for all with each of us paying an affordable premium. But as we live longer, we are increasingly likely to require the use of high-tech diagnostic tools, surgical procedures, and expensive radiation and chemotherapy to keep us alive. This means that the cost of healthcare will inevitably rise, and thus the premium payments must also rise. What if the government paid for healthcare? Regardless of who pays, the grim reality is that the cost will go up. If we expect government to pay for healthcare, the reality is that we must expect to pay higher taxes to keep the government solvent.

We expect fixes for injuries and cures for diseases regardless of how we choose to treat our bodies and whether or not we can afford to pay for healthcare. A high percentage of adults in developed countries are overweight, which lends them more susceptible to diseases such as diabetes and other ailments associated with obesity or decreased mobility. Those who smoke increase their risk of cancer and lung diseases and those who participate in extreme sports increase their risk of breaking bones or worse. Those who choose not to take personal responsibility to live a healthy or low risk lifestyle expect the same level of care as everyone else.

Regardless of how we treat our bodies, we expect the healthcare system to take care of us when something goes wrong. In reality, the cost of healthcare is often increased by our choices of unhealthy or risky living. That increased cost has to be paid by someone; by higher insurance premiums or by further drawing on the unsustainable Medicare or Medicaid programs or other national healthcare systems.

We expect to retire at age sixty-five or sooner with a lifetime income sufficient to maintain our pre-retirement standard of living. We expect to draw Social Security payments for as long as we live, no matter how long that turns out to be. After all, we paid into the program throughout our working years and we rightfully feel entitled to benefit from it. The problem is that Social Security was established during a time (1935) when life expectancy was much shorter (fifty-eight for men and sixty-two for women) than it is today, and although it has been adjusted some, it is still not designed for current actuarial realities.

Politicians are well aware of the problems with Social Security, but they are reluctant to fix them because they fear they will not be reelected if they vote to reduce benefits or increase the age at which benefits can be drawn. I suspect the main lobbying group politicians fear on this issue is the American Association of Retired Persons, although this puzzles me because it would seem more logical to me that an organization such as AARP would be leading the charge for fixing the problem. At any rate, the grim reality is that Social Security cannot meet expectations without significant overhaul, either by increasing the retirement age, decreasing benefits, or increasing payments by those still working or a combination of these. Barring significant changes, the Social Security program could be bankrupt within a few decades. The same situation applies to the Medicare program.

In addition to the fact that people are living longer the other problem with Social Security and Medicare, which depend on enough young workers to support the elderly, is the declining birth rates that have resulted in fewer people of working age to pay into the programs. The population replacement rate, that is the birth rate that is necessary to keep a population at the same level (without immigration or emigration), is about 2.1 births per woman in most developed countries. Currently over 110 countries, including the United States, have estimated birth rates at or below 2.1 (estimates for 2016 from the US Central Intelligence Agency's World Factbook).

In underdeveloped nations the replacement rate is considerably higher than 2.1 because children are less likely to live to adulthood where access to medical care and good nutrition is limited. However, even in underdeveloped nations birth rates are declining.

Declining birth rates worldwide have both ecological and economic implications. From an ecological perspective, birth rates declining below replacement rates imply that the world's population will stabilize and begin to drop in the foreseeable future, perhaps to a sustainable level before resources are depleted. Thus from an ecological perspective declining birth rates should be seen as a good thing. The opposite is true from an economic perspective, at least in the context of the grow or die paradigm. Economic growth will most certainly decline as populations shrink and age. This is a clear indication that economic growth is unsustainable not just from an ecological perspective but from a demographic one as well.

Those of us who have money in tax-sheltered retirement funds with assets in the stock market expect those funds to increase steadily at a rate higher than could be had with savings accounts at our local banks. We are constantly being told that the stock market steadily rises, in spite of occasional "corrections" or dips in the upward-marching curve. Most financial advisers stress investing in the stock market but put little emphasis on savings; indeed I wonder if most people understand the difference between saving and investing.

What is the difference? My opinion is that savings is money you set aside in a secure place where it is readily available for unexpected expenses or for things you know you will need like new tires for your car or a new roof on your house. Investments on the other hand are funds that you can do without if you have to; money that you can put at risk with the possibility of returns greater than you could achieve from a savings account at a bank. Now, if these definitions applied to the majority of people, those who don't make enough money to put any at risk means that most people should not have money in the stock market. Historically, this has been the case, but since the unusual bull market of the 1990s, the general public has become enamored with stocks and egged on by financial advisors and the news media, many people have borrowed money to buy stocks.

Borrowing money takes many forms, the most common being credit card debt that is not totally paid off with each monthly statement, auto loans, and home mortgages. If a person has money at risk in the stock market while paying interest on any of the above, then I would argue that that person is borrowing money in order to speculate in the stock market. It's an indirect relationship to be sure, but just as risky as taking out a direct loan to buy stocks. In short, our expectation that the stock market will always trend higher is offset by the reality that it is risky to bet the farm on it.

Those of us who own real estate, whether it is a farm, a home, or land that we have bought for speculation, have come to expect the value of that property to steadily rise. Indeed, since there is no more land being made and there is an ever-increasing population competing for that land, it seems like a given that land values will increase. But as the recent housing bubble illustrated, land values can fluctuate up or down, at least in the short term. And depending on the location, the long-term trend may be down, for example in areas where manufacturing jobs have disappeared the population may decrease and property values decline. Likewise, in areas where severe and unusual flooding has devastated homes and businesses, property values may stagnate or decline because of the perceived risk of future flooding.

Many of us believe that taxes are too high and thus expect to pay lower taxes in the future. Indeed, a significant percentage of politicians promise to lower taxes while maintaining services at current levels. In reality, such promises are designed to get politicians elected or reelected, and are not designed to solve problems. Many of these same politicians promise that cutting taxes will help stimulate the economy and increase growth. In reality, taxes tend to be higher in more densely populated areas, so creating more growth is likely to fuel the need for more services and hence higher taxes rather than lower ones. Another hard reality is that more tax revenue is needed, not less, if our government is ever going to reduce its burdensome debt.

Many people complain that there are too many government regulations, but in reality, there is a direct connection between population density and the need for laws and regulations. Common sense holds that the denser the population the greater the likelihood that what one person does will negatively impact someone else, and thus we need more regulations (and government employees to administer and enforce them) to protect our individual interests. We have lower speed limits and more traffic lights in densely populated areas for sound safety reasons. Noise restrictions are also a result of the need to protect ones neighbors from the loud parties or other sources of sounds unpleasant to other people. Zoning regulations are designed to separate incompatible land uses and considered essential in densely populated areas but generally not necessary where population density is low. The grim reality is that population growth drives the need for bigger government to administer and enforce more regulations.

We have come to expect unlimited clean water at the turn of a spigot. But water is not an infinite resource. As population density builds, it becomes increasingly difficult and expensive to locate and tap into new sources of water and conflicts over water rights are likely to increase. As I write this there is an unresolved dispute among the states of Georgia, Florida, and Alabama over how to allocate water from the Chattahoochee River. This dispute has been simmering for over twenty years. During dry periods citizens are asked or even mandated to use less water by restricting outdoor watering, washing vehicles, etc. The reality is that water resources are limited and we can expect more restrictions on water use and more cost for the water we use as population density increases.

We have also come to expect to fuel our cars, heat, and air-condition our homes and have all the electricity we need to run more and better appliances without any thought about how growth affects fuel supplies. The grim reality is that most of the energy we use comes from non-renewable fossil fuels and our use of them is unsustainable even at current population levels. The more the population grows, the sooner these fossil fuels will be depleted.

So we see that many of our expectations for a brighter future for our generation and those that follow are based on a belief that economic growth is the essential key to meeting those expectations. However, if we are willing to closely examine the foundation of our economic growth, we must reach the logical conclusion that the foundation is weak and that growth is unsustainable. The grim reality is that we cannot count on economic growth to sustain our higher expectations for future generations.

We have come to expect to do more with less because of science and technology, but that trend can only go so far and the more efficient our machines are the more unskilled workers there are without meaningful employment. The reality is that technology is often a double edged sword; it may be good for the company producing a product and good for the consumer because of the lower price of that product, but many low-income people still may not be able to benefit because their jobs have been replaced by the technology and therefore don't have the resources to afford the product.

While I'm on the subject of doing more with less, let's consider the need to grow more food on less land. Presently the earth's 7.5 billion people are fed (granted many of them are not well fed) with food grown on about 11 percent of the world's dry land plus seafood harvests and home gardens. As farmland is gradually gobbled up by urban development it becomes a real challenge to produce more food on less land. Will the world's farmers be able to feed the additional two billion people forecasted to inhabit the earth by the year 2050 with food grown on perhaps only 9 percent of the dry land. Clearly, the grim reality is that even if this feat can be accomplished in 2050, it seems unlikely that it can be sustained much beyond then as we continue to deplete the resources that modern agriculture depends on.

CHAPTER 10

RELEARNING NATURE

I have already mentioned that our long-ago ancestors must have been intimately familiar with the natural world around them because such familiarity would have been essential for their survival. Not so with most modern humans in the developed world. Nowadays, the majority of the world's population lives in urban areas where our dependence on the services provided by nature is far from obvious. Especially in the more affluent nations, where job specialization has required most individuals to focus on making a living within a narrow field of expertise, it has become easy for people to ignore the natural world. Indeed, many people who live in urban areas are at least somewhat fearful of natural environments, especially those without developed trails and nearby services such as motels and restaurants.

One result of job specialization is that more and more people spend most of their time indoors. They work in factories, offices, or other buildings for eight or more hours each weekday and then go home and spend their nonworking hours indoors watching television or focusing on other electronic devices. Most of those who do spend time outdoors are playing golf or other sports that require an artificially landscaped playing field that may or may not even faintly resemble a natural area. In short, so many modern humans spend most of their lives on pavement or other artificial or landscaped surfaces and in climate controlled environments that there is little wonder they have limited knowledge of or appreciation for the natural environment that sustains them.

How we humans see ourselves in relation to the natural world must surely affect our attitude toward that natural world. We modern humans have become so focused on our business interests, economic issues and other man-made things that affect our ability to make a living that most of us rarely stop to consider how we fit into the natural order of things or what our responsibilities might be in order to be stewards of the natural world.

Although we may wish to ignore it, other creatures are in fact our kin—we all sprang from common ancestors over the course of millennia. The fact that humans have come to dominate the earth and its resources does not give us the right to trash the habitats of other creatures. On the contrary, our ability to dominate the earth lays on our shoulders the heavy responsibility to take care of it, for by taking care of the needs of other species we in fact take care of our own needs as well. Protecting the earth's ecosystems from the destruction that we have the ability to wreak is the only way to ensure our own survival. Developing a sense of kinship with the rest of the world's living things is indeed in our own self-interest.

I believe there is a critical need for modern humans to get back in touch with their natural environment; essentially relearn the kinds of things our ancestors knew and more. The more we can learn about how we fit in our ecosystem, the better we will be prepared to make responsible decisions regarding issues pertaining to growth. In the United States, we have an abundance of opportunities to educate ourselves and our children outside the formal classroom setting. In this chapter, I will explore some available opportunities that I am familiar with.

No matter where you live in the United States, there is probably some public land near your home that is managed in a relatively natural state. Such places include national, state, and local parks, national and state forests, and even land managed by non-governmental organizations such as The Nature Conservancy and other science or conservation groups. Visit their websites to get basic information such as visiting hours, fees, and driving directions. Visit offices and ask questions about trails to walk, wildlife you might see, and whether or not specific educational programs are offered. Many such areas have educational displays that highlight unique features of local ecosystems that will help you gain basic knowledge. Ask questions—remember that the only dumb questions are those that don't get asked.

Parents, look for youth programs that get children involved in fun and educational outdoor activities. Boy Scout and Girl Scout troops, if well led and supervised by knowledgeable and caring adults, can be great opportunities to get children involved and curious about the natural world. My son benefitted greatly from his experiences with his Boy Scout troop and still talks about memorable out-ings some twenty-five years later.

Georgia state parks are scattered throughout the state so that at least one is just a short distance from most state residents, and the same is true in many other states. Many amenities offered by state parks, such as tennis courts, swimming beaches and golf courses do not necessarily lend themselves to environmental education, but most state parks include undeveloped land with some maintained hiking trails that beckon visitors to explore beyond the obvious man made attractions. Don't be afraid to explore such areas. Maps are usually available to guide you and many trails include informational signs that explain simple ecosystems or identify various species of trees or geological features.

If you are fortunate enough to live near a national park or national recreation area, you can take advantage of many of the same types of nature-related activities that you would find at state parks except the national parks, due to bet-ter funding and higher public demand, are more likely to employ rangers that are knowledgeable in a broader range of ecosystem issues. Since national parks are usually much larger than state parks they will likely have a broader range of ecosystem types to explore. Park publications will help guide you to unique areas and ranger-guided programs will likely be available.

Many state wildlife management agencies place a great deal of emphasis on environmental education. Project Wild is a nationwide wildlife-focused education program for K–12 educators and their students. It is sponsored by state wildlife management agencies throughout the nation and is based on the premise that young people and their educators have a vital interest in learning about the natural world. Project Wild emphasizes the intrinsic value of wildlife and uses that as a focal point to address the need for human beings to develop as responsible citizens. The mission of Project Wild is to assist learners of any age in developing awareness, knowledge, skills, and commitment to result in informed decisions, responsible behavior, and constructive actions concerning wildlife and the environment upon which all life depends. Parents can encourage the use of Project Wild in their children's schools as a means of learning basic ecosystem principles.

Georgia has both wildlife management areas and public fishing areas that cater not just to hunters and fishers, but welcome non-consumptive users as well. Managers of these areas welcome the opportunity to answer questions and most are prepared to schedule group educational programs when asked. Even if you do not feel comfortable with the idea of hunting you can still take advantage of these large tracts of public land that are managed for multiple uses. Look for your state's wildlife management agency's website to begin learning about outdoor programs and opportunities that are available near you.

National forests are open to the public and offer excellent resources for exploring various types of ecosystems and practicing outdoor skills. These areas, managed by the United States Forest Service, encompass some 193 million acres across the country. Some 80 percent of these lands are in the western United States, but most eastern states also have national forests. When I worked as a fisheries biologist I had the opportunity to interact with many Forest Service personnel and became familiar with many of the forest management issues in eastern national forests. Typically these lands are managed for multiple uses but the primary emphasis is on promoting ecosystem health and biological productivity while encouraging low impact recreation.

Georgia's Chattahoochee and Oconee national forests span over 865,000 acres across twenty-six counties, mostly in the northern part of the state. Most of these lands were purchased by the federal government in the early part of the twentieth century; at the time they were mostly cut over and eroding timber lands that few people wanted. Today these lands offer over 850 miles of trails, dozens of campgrounds, picnic areas, and thousands of miles of clear freshwater streams. These public lands are great areas for hunting, fishing, picnicking, hiking, and simply enjoying nature's beauty.

If you are new to exploring large tracts of public land, I encourage you to take full advantage of developed and marked trail systems. But to fully enjoy undeveloped land, once you are comfortable using the trails, get off the trails where you can better appreciate the plants and animals and different ecosystems you will likely encounter. Note that you will find some areas where signs ask you to stay on marked trials, usually to protect delicate habitat or keep you away from dangerous areas such as cliffs for example. Before you decide to do any off-trail hiking get a map and learn to use it. Use a compass if you need to. Plenty of books and internet websites are available to help you learn how to get around safely in the outdoors. Relatively inexpensive GPS systems or GPS apps for smartphones are also readily available to guide you. Take a gradual approach; don't venture far from the trail on your first attempt or until you become experienced.

Wherever you go in the outdoors, please respect the environment by not leaving your trash. A good motto to follow is "leave only footprints and take only pictures." If you carry a bottle of water or a canned drink with you don't throw the empty container on the ground when you finish it. If the drink wasn't too heavy to carry into the woods, then the empty container certainly isn't too heavy to carry out. Personally, I get some satisfaction in carrying out a bit of trash that someone else has left in the woods and knowing that I left the area a bit cleaner than I found it.

You may want to take an interest in cultivating and caring for plants as a way of learning about natural things. Many cities have community garden space that can be rented for a nominal fee. Or perhaps there is a vacant lot nearby that could be used, with permission, to grow things. Don't know where to begin? Most states have university extension offices that are available to answer questions about horticulture and many free brochures, both in print and on the internet are available to address specific topics about soils, vegetable gardening, fruit growing and many other topics. County extension agents are not just for farmers; in fact, many of them spend most of their time helping city dwellers.

The university extension offices have another helpful program called master gardeners. These are citizen volunteers that have taken an intensive horticulture course and volunteer in their communities to help educate citizens about natural resources and promote gardening of various types. Many master gardeners work with local schools to maintain junior master gardener programs that teach young people about gardening and other related topics such as the importance of pollinators, composting and beneficial insects. Junior master gardener programs demonstrate that food does not originate in grocery stores, and encourage students to expand their knowledge beyond simply growing plants.

Consider joining a garden club as a way to meet others interested in plants and interested in sharing their knowledge with others. Garden clubs generally do not have large memberships, so it is easy to get to know people. These clubs usually invite speakers with knowledge of various horticulture or outdoor subjects to give presentations at regular meetings. Call your local county extension office for information about garden clubs in your area.

If you take my advice to get to better know the outdoor environment, you will probably want to learn some basic ecology. I have already devoted a chapter to ecological issues, but I wish here to offer the reader some additional basic principles that will be helpful to carry to the field as you expand your exploration of the outdoors. If you are not ready to delve further into ecology, feel free to move on to the next chapter.

Natural processes operate in a cyclical manner and there are several readily describable cycles that anyone who takes an interest in the natural environment should be aware of. Most of these cycles are rather complex, but for the intended purpose of introductory material, they can be simplified. Whether considered in a simple or complex manner, a basic knowledge of natural cycles should give anyone a better understanding of how everything is connected in the natural environment that we all depend on.

Let's start with the oxygen cycle. I suspect that most adults already know that green plants produce oxygen via the process of photosynthesis and that animals need that oxygen to survive. Animals breathe in oxygen and exhale carbon dioxide, which plants then use along with water to supply the basic building blocks to construct their cells. This is a basic cycle that applies primarily to atmospheric oxygen and dissolved oxygen in bodies of water and the process of photosynthesis is the main driver of this cycle. Photosynthesis is the single most important factor that is responsible for life on earth as we know it.

It bears mentioning that the majority of the earth's oxygen is tied up in rocks and minerals in the form of silicates and oxides. This oxygen can be extracted by certain plants and animals and thus released back into the atmosphere, but the process is extremely slow and is a minor contributor to the oxygen cycle.

Closely related to the oxygen cycle is the carbon cycle. Carbon is the main element of organic or biological compounds and is thus essential to life on earth. Carbon is cycled among the atmosphere, oceans, sediments, and living things and the natural flow of carbon among these locations is relatively balanced except for human activities that are adding additional carbon to the atmosphere and oceans. Carbon in the form of carbon dioxide is cycled out of the atmosphere and into terrestrial and aquatic plants by photosynthesis which uses carbon dioxide and water to build plant cells as described above for the oxygen cycle. Animals obtain carbon by eating plants and while they are alive they cycle much of it back into the atmosphere through respiration.

Both plants and animals die and decay and become part of the soil and eventually some of their remains wind up in sediments that ultimately become rock or hydrocarbon deposits such as coal or oil. Limestone is a good example of carbon stored in sedimentary rock as calcium carbonate, which was formed primarily by the shells of marine organisms. Carbon stored in such geologic deposits can remain undisturbed for millions of years. This geologic carbon can eventually be released back into the atmosphere by volcanic eruptions or by extraction and burning of fossil fuels by humans. Much of the carbon dioxide released from burning fossil fuels is not absorbed by plants or the ocean and thus remains in the atmosphere. The concentration of carbon dioxide in the atmosphere has increased by over 40 percent since the beginning of the industrial revolution.

I will begin a description of the nitrogen cycle by stating that the air we breathe is approximately 80 percent nitrogen, existing there in its inorganic form as nitrogen gas (N_2). Ironically, however, this vast pool of nitrogen is largely unavailable to living things until it is converted into a usable form—a process known as fixation. Some of this nitrogen gets fixed by lightning strikes, but most of the conversion takes place by nitrogen-fixing bacteria. These bacteria use unique enzymes to combine nitrogen with hydrogen to form ammonia, which the bacteria then convert into other nitrogen compounds that can be used by plants.

Plants absorb nitrogen from the soil in the form of ammonium ions and nitrates and use these compounds to produce amino acids and chlorophyll. Animals obtain nitrogen in the form of amino acids by eating plants or other animals. Amino acids are the building blocks of proteins and are thus essential for building muscle tissue. When an animal or plant dies soil bacteria or fungi convert the nitrogen in them back into ammonium ions where they are again available for plant growth. Nitrogen is returned to the atmosphere by denitrifying bacteria that convert soil nitrates back into the gaseous form.

The water cycle, also known as the hydrologic cycle, is the means whereby water moves among the atmosphere, the ocean, ice, freshwater rivers, streams, and lakes and underground aquifers (groundwater). Freshwater rivers and streams flow into the ocean where some of it evaporates to form rainclouds which replenish the land with purified water. Since ocean levels stay relatively constant (except for gradually rising due to melting glaciers), the total amount of evaporation from ocean and lake surfaces equals the total volume of all streams flowing into the oceans plus the volume of rainwater that falls directly on the oceans. That is a lot of evaporation!

Depending on the amount and intensity of rainfall, most of it may flow quickly into streams or it may gradually soak into the ground. Some of the rainwater will gradually or relatively quickly, depending on local geology, enter underground aquifers where it may reemerge as springs which contribute to stream flow.

Snowfall at higher elevations and in the polar regions may be stored as packed snow or glacial ice, which will gradually release its water during the warmer months, or may add to the depth of glaciers and not become melt water for decades or centuries. Water absorbed by soil becomes available to plants, which require it for photosynthesis. Only a small amount of the water taken up by plant roots is used for growth and metabolism. The vast majority of this water is transferred to the atmosphere by evaporation from leaves, stems and flowers. So the hydrologic cycle sees water as solid, liquid or gas (vapor), depending on variables such as temperature and pressure.

Notice from the above descriptions of the various cycles how they are intertwined. Oxygen is somehow involved in the other cycles, and thus is part of them. Carbon is the main element of biological compounds and thus essential to life as we know it. The nitrogen cycle provides plant nutrients and interacts with oxygen in various processes. Water is the common compound that allows all the other cycles to operate efficiently.

Now we can be certain that our prehistoric ancestors knew nothing about these cycles that are essential to the survival of life on earth, and indeed there was no need for them to know more than the bare essentials of how to meet their daily needs for food, water and shelter. We modern humans, however, need to have some knowledge of these essential workings of our natural environment because we now have the ability to disrupt them in ways that could be detrimental to our well-being.

We have already altered the carbon cycle by destroying forests and burning fossil fuels, resulting in a 40 percent increase in carbon dioxide in the atmosphere. We have interfered with the hydrologic cycle by pumping water out of aquifers faster than it can be replenished.

We humans have also altered the nitrogen cycle by intensive culture of legumes such as alfalfa and clover, the manufacture of chemical fertilizers from fossil fuels, and by emissions from vehicles and industrial plants. These activities have more than doubled the annual transfer of nitrogen into biological forms. Nitrous oxide is a byproduct of man's activities that acts as a catalyst in the destruction of atmospheric ozone, and it is also the third largest contributor to greenhouse gases after carbon dioxide and methane. In lakes and rivers, excess nitrogen causes over-fertilization (eutrophication) which can rob these water bodies of oxygen and deplete aquatic life. An ocean "dead zone" in the Gulf of Mexico at the mouth of the Mississippi River is a well-known example of excess nutrients having depleted oxygen in a very large area.

I have heard it said, and I tend to agree, that basic economics should be a required college course. I would also argue that basic ecology should be a required course, especially for those who major in economics. I would go one step further and suggest a required course for both majors that would deal with the obvious conflicts between economic growth and ecosystem stability as a way of getting these two disciplines to better communicate with each other and perhaps help move the world a bit closer to a sustainable condition.

CHAPTER 11

RETHINKING GOVERNMENT

I spent a career that dealt primarily with the practical application of ecological principles to freshwater fish habitats, but it also included some study of the impacts of human activities on ecosystems. It is clear to me that the current growth equals progress paradigm must be challenged because it almost totally ignores ecosystem needs. It must be challenged because the quality of life for future generations depends on the health of our ecosystems and biosphere far more than on how much money is circulating in the economy.

The planning process used by governments must shift away from the "more is always better" philosophy demanded by the growth equals progress paradigm to a philosophy that understands the need to maintain a healthy ecosystem and the need to use resources in a sustainable manner. In short, government planning should be more ecosystem-based and less economics-based.

Government planning processes also need to be more long-range and more considerate of the laws of nature and actuarial realities. Currently long range planning for most politicians seems to reach about as far into the future as the next election. Once a politician gets in office, he or she needs to focus more on solving problems and less on raising money for the next campaign. A politician focuses on staying in office; a statesman focuses on solving problems. We currently have too many politicians and too few statesmen.

Many will argue that the way we have always planned has worked well, and therefore, there is no need to change. But circumstances have changed. Outside of colonizing Mars, we have run out of new frontiers to expand into. Our planning process must also change if we are to maintain our present quality of life or have any hope of improving conditions for future generations.

Not only have we run out of frontiers, it is also clear that the resources we have used to support our growth are far from inexhaustible and indeed are rapidly being used up. As a young fisheries biologist, I thought there was no way humans could overharvest fish in our vast oceans (the Pacific Ocean is 64 million square miles in area and up to seven miles deep). However, it is now common knowledge that many ocean fish stocks have been severely depleted using gear and techniques unimagined a half century ago. We also know that much of the world's vast timber resources are being harvested at unsustainable levels and that fossil fuels that required millions of years to develop are being rapidly depleted.

The evidence of unsustainable resource use is abundant worldwide. If we can step back and view things outside our growth equals progress paradigm we can see abundant examples locally as well. Most people call them problems: how to supply water for future populations, how to dispose of wastes safely, how to keep our air and water clean. These are but a few examples but they are not problems at all; only symptoms of a real and major change in circumstances that demand our immediate and thoughtful attention.

Growth, be it economic or population, can have either positive or negative consequences, or both, depending on the circumstances. Because the economy is a subset of the ecosystem, government policy needs to recognize the resource limits to growth and adopt policies that discourage growth that resources cannot support. In other words, government policy should take an ecosystem based approach to planning for the future. It seems reasonable that certain areas of the world might benefit from some increase in population in order to support better infrastructure or a greater variety of employment opportunities, for example. It seems just as reasonable to think that some very densely populated areas could benefit from economic growth if it results in a qualitative improvement in the lives of the less affluent and if it could be achieved without further population increase.

Local governments tend to promote growth by various means when they might better serve their constituents by adopting growth-neutral policies. The various incentives given to attract new industry (and more people), such as installing water and sewer lines into undeveloped areas and buying land for industrial parks, often burns public money that would be better spent serving existing residents.

Government officials claim that attracting industry broadens the tax base, resulting in lower taxes for homeowners. While this may be true to some extent in areas where population density is very low, tax rates generally rise as population density increases. Assessed property values also rise as population density increases and this further increases the amount property owners pay in taxes. Sales taxes are also usually higher in more densely populated areas. Rents also rise with increasing population density, so people who do not own land also pay more for growth. Local governments would better serve their citizenry by acknowledging these negative aspects of growth.

Government policy needs to recognize the concept of optimum as it applies to human population density. Understanding that more is not always better would lead to a recognition of the connection between population density and resource availability, and hence to a recognition that declining living standards are inevitable as competition for resources escalates.

Now the concept of optimum population density is not easy to determine when it comes to human populations, but it surely is an important concept just the same. With current human populations and living standards supported to such a great extent by the depletion of energy and water resources, the concept of optimum needs to be thought of in light of what level of resource use can reasonably be considered sustainable. As a means of beginning the process of determining optimum population, government officials could actually ask citizens for their opinions about how big their communities should be, how much traffic congestion they want, how much more, if any, they want to pay in additional taxes to support the long-term consequences of growth.

Government tax policy is an area that seems ripe for changes that would move the nation toward a sustainable future. Our federal income tax system is clearly broken, and it is time to fix it. I am not proposing a major over-haul of tax policy, although I do believe such things as the Fair Tax, a flat tax, and national sales or value-added taxes should be more thoroughly debated as possible alternatives to the current complex income tax system. Perhaps the current system could be simplified by removing most of the deductions and loopholes but if our current taxation system remains in place, I believe a few simple changes need to be considered.

At the federal level, the most critical need is to take fiscal responsibility by balancing the budget so the nation can gradually emerge from its massive debt. I believe this can best be done through a combination of spending cuts and tax increases. This is a highly charged political issue and I prefer not to discuss politics in this book but certain facts need to be addressed.

Readily available data make it clear that the national debt began spiraling out of control in the decade of the 1980s, when the total debt tripled. This was a direct result of the failure of a theory known then as trickle-down economics, which essentially held that tax cuts, especially for the wealthiest individuals, would result in more money used to create jobs and stimulate the economy to the point where tax revenues would actually increase. Although it quickly became obvious that trickle-down economics would not work there are still many people today who seem to believe that the theory is valid because they continue to advocate lower taxes for the rich to stimulate the economy.

Shortly after the dawn of the twenty-first century more tax cuts for the wealthy brought on a doubling of the national debt. The nation essentially paid for two wars, an increase in Social Security benefits and new government programs by borrowing money. Then, with the nation in a severe recession the other political party began spending large amounts of money that it had to borrow in order to "create jobs" and pay for a massive but little understood national healthcare program. When one political party was in power it famously proclaimed that "deficits don't matter," but as soon as it was the minority party its members started screaming about how the nation was going bankrupt, while at the same time refusing to consider eliminating the previous tax cuts for the wealthy.

Such political behavior is disgraceful, to put it mildly. We need fewer politicians and more statesmen. Recall the closing sentence in the Declaration of Independence in which the fifty-six signers, who were for the most part very wealthy men, pledged "to each other our lives, our fortunes and our sacred honor." Contrast that with the attitude of most wealthy people today who seem bent on protecting their fortunes by avoiding paying any more taxes than they absolutely have to. Perhaps many wealthy people in our modern era have no "sacred honor" or maybe no honor at all. It seems many wealthy people would rather see the United States go bankrupt than use some of their wealth to help control the runaway debt.

Both political parties have clearly shown a lack of will to cut spending on entitlement programs, so increasing tax revenue seems to be the only solution to the nation's growing fiscal crisis. If that is the case, and if we continue to depend on income taxes as the major source of Federal revenue, what is the best way to increase tax revenue? I don't know the answer to that question, but I have a few ideas that I think are worth considering.

We have often heard that income tax cuts result in increased revenue. Widely respected columnists, talk show hosts and some members of Congress often point to tax cuts during the Kennedy, Reagan, G. W. Bush and even the Coolidge administrations, saying that in each case federal tax revenues increased in the following years. Since this sounds too good to be true, it bears looking into in more detail.

The Kennedy-era tax cut took effect in 1964, when the top tax bracket was cut from 91% to 70% and tax rates on lower income brackets were cut by two or more percentage points. Tax receipts had been steadily increasing for five years prior to 1964 and they continued to increase at a slightly higher rate in the following years.

Does simply looking at tax receipts oversimplify the issue? For example, if the size of the economy is steadily increasing one would expect that tax revenues might grow even with lower tax rates. Tax receipts as a percentage of GDP fell slightly in 1964, but gradually recovered and rose to slightly above pre-1964 levels for a few years. Bottom line: it would be hard to argue that the lower tax rates beginning in 1964 did not have at least a slight positive effect on tax receipts. Even after the 1964 cut, however, top earners were still taxed at a 70% rate, much higher than today's top rates.

The next tax cuts came in 1982, when the top bracket was reduced from 70% to 50% and lower income brackets were again cut by a few percentage points. Then in 1986 a major overhaul of the tax code reduced the number of brackets from fifteen to five, with the top bracket at only 38.5% beginning in 1987. If tax cuts really increase revenue, these cuts should certainly have demonstrated that effect, so let's see what happened.

In the fifteen years prior to 1982, income tax revenue rose at an average rate of about 10% each year. In the next fifteen years, revenue rose at an average annual rate of less than 6%. So the claim that revenue increased after the so-called Reagan tax cuts is misleading. Yes, revenue continued to increase each year compared to the previous year, but more revenue would have been collected had the tax rates not been cut. Clearly the claim that tax cuts increase revenue is false and those who continue to make that claim are doing the nation a disservice.

The 1980s also saw huge increases in annual budget deficits, resulting in the national debt nearly tripling during that decade. One might expect increased deficit spending alone to increase tax revenue because of the stimulating effect such spending would have on the economy. However, any such benefit was more than offset by the decreased contribution of the highest-income earners to the total tax receipts.

Following the Bush tax cuts in the early 2000s, tax receipts actually dropped for a few years, but then only saw an average increase of less than 1 percent per year from 2001 through 2009. Most importantly, tax receipts as a percentage of GDP continued to lag.

What about tax increases? If the myth were true that tax cuts result in revenue increases, then it follows that tax increases should result in decreased revenue. Not so. The tax increases effective in 1991 and 1993 were followed by an average annual gain in revenue of 7% from 1991 through 2000.

The logical conclusion of this analysis is that those who still propose cutting taxes, especially for the top income earners, as a solution to the growing fiscal crisis facing our nation are clearly out of touch with reality. It is high time for serious debate about how this nation can fund its operating budget and especially the ever more expensive entitlement programs, and which of those programs it can indeed afford. If we remain with the current income tax system then raising taxes on those most able to pay appears to be the best solution. As the famous bank robber Willie Sutton allegedly said when asked why he robbed banks: "Because that's where the money is."

Now it seems that one political party is adamant that spending must be cut to balance the budget while the other party is adamant that taxes must be raised. It seems obvious to me that both steps must be taken. The party that demands spending cuts had ample opportunity to do so when it was in power, but it not only failed to balance the budget but increased the debt substantially. The party that wants to raise taxes has largely failed, at least recently, to demonstrate a desire to cut spending. In short, neither of the major political parties appears to be taking the national debt seriously, and judging from polls reported by the media, the national debt is not even a major concern of the general public. I believe that is very unfortunate.

Politicians who advocate spending cuts have made little headway at least partly because they have failed to come up with plans that cut a significant amount of spending while at the same time garnering sufficient support from their colleagues. Spending cuts also pose a dilemma to politicians who advocate them because of outcries from those who see the cuts as affecting programs or services dear to them. Such cuts are usually aimed at programs seen as wasteful, at least from one or more politician's point of view. A program or service may seem wasteful to a politician if eliminating it would not significantly affect his constituents, but the same program or service may seem essential to another politician whose constituents depend to a greater extent on it and make their voices heard. I hate to repeat myself, but we need fewer politicians and more statesmen.

Protecting pet programs from spending cuts is often a good example of how politicians tend to put less emphasis on the national interest compared to local interests. Thus spending cuts are much more difficult to implement than many of those who advocate them seem to think. Money-losing federal programs are also difficult to get rid of, and thus fall into the same category as spending cuts.

One money-losing federal program that I am some-what familiar with and seems ripe for overhauling is the generation of electricity at government owned dams. The electricity produced by these dams must by law be sold at the cost of producing it. However, at least two flaws in the system guarantee that the government actually loses money on the electricity it generates. First of all, the power is not sold directly by the agencies producing it (primarily the Army Corps of Engineers and the Bureau of Reclamation). The power is instead sold via contract negotiated by regional marketing agencies which have their own separate budgets, resulting in added cost to the government since the cost of marketing is not part of the production cost.

The second flaw lies in the way the power is sold by the marketing agencies. The power is sold via contracts, which are drawn up in advance of production. The contracts are for the amount of power a facility historically produces and at historic production cost. However, if the facility cannot meet the contract obligation (during a dry year for example when there is not enough water to generate the contracted amount of electricity) then the government must buy power on the open market from more expensive sources and sell it at the lower contract price. During years when more power is produced than the contract specifies, the surplus still must be sold at the contract price.

This situation could be fixed by changing the law to require power to be sold at market value. This should enable the individual generating facilities to negotiate prices directly with the private power companies, thus eliminating the power marketing agencies (the middle men) and guaranteeing an operational profit for the generating facilities. Because hydroelectricity is relatively cheap to produce and most of it can be sold at a premium price when demand is at its peak the potential profit for the federal treasury is significant.

Now if the government made money on its power production many people's electric bill would probably increase by some small amount. And the private power companies and rural electric cooperatives would cry foul at the prospect of paying market value for a product they have grown accustomed to getting at a subsidized rate. But it seems foolish to subsidize an industry that can do quite well without government assistance.

Although trickle-down economics was a proven failure, many politicians still advocate the concept. Now, it does not take a genius to understand that if cutting taxes actually increased revenue both political parties would have agreed to cut taxes to practically zero a long time ago and the government would now have all the revenue it needs for whatever programs either party wants. It is time to abandon such fanciful ideas and use some common sense to figure out an optimal taxation policy that moves the nation toward fiscal responsibility.

Balancing the federal budget would not only decrease the risk of national bankruptcy, by setting a good example it would also encourage citizens to make more effort to balance their own budgets. Another way to encourage citizens to save money instead of borrowing it would be to change tax policy on mortgage interest deductions. Currently home mortgage interest deductions are allowed for both first and second homes for mortgages totaling up to $1 million. Such deductions should be capped at a much lower level (perhaps $200,000) and should be allowed only for a family's primary residence. Conversely, allowing a tax exemption for interest earned on savings accounts instead of taxing that interest would help encourage people to save money for a rainy day.

Another growth-neutral tax policy would be to limit the number of dependents claimed on tax returns. Such a policy might discourage people from having children they can't afford to take care of but it should not have a significant impact on family planning among financially sound households.

Anyone depending on government benefits should be required to sign a statement acknowledging that they understand that they won't receive benefits for additional children. This is a common sense approach to managing entitlements; taxpayers should not be expected to support children that the beneficiary of public funds cannot afford to raise. Just as a private individual would expect someone he/she is helping not to make their situation worse while being helped, so should government assistance programs have the same expectations. Such a policy likely would also help contribute to breaking the cycle of poverty that has resulted in multigenerational dependence on government support.

Government should not plan for growth as if growth is inevitable; government should plan for sustainability. Local government "leaders" are especially prone to deny their deliberate efforts to promote growth by saying things like "growth is going to come whether we like it or not, so we have to plan for it." Instead, why not say "growth is not in the driver's seat and we need to manage for what is best for our citizens in the long run." Such a change in outlook would allow leaders to evaluate both positive and negative aspects of growth, determine who benefits and who pays, and seek ways for growth to pay for the additional infrastructure it requires instead of current residents paying for infrastructure to attract growth that most citizens might not even want.

Many citizens today express a strong desire for smaller government and less intrusive laws and regulations imposed on business, industry and individuals. However, it seems obvious that the need for more restrictive regulations is a direct result of population growth. As a matter of common sense, the greater the population density, the more likely it is that what one person or business does will affect his neighbor in a negative way. Thus we need regulations to prevent soil erosion from construction projects to protect downstream property owners and public water supplies. With a growing population comes the need for more roads, more infrastructure, more traffic signals (and public resources to maintain them) to keep roads safe with the increased traffic caused by growth. Zoning laws are increasingly needed as populations increase. There are many other examples of how government needs to grow along with population growth (think air and water quality regulations and the monitoring that goes with them, and emissions controls on vehicles). This list could go on, but I hope I have made my point by now. It is simply not realistic to expect a shrinking government in the face of population growth, yet many folks who decry government regulations are the very ones who advocate "growing the economy."

One problem with our representative form of government that hinders our thinking about sustainability is that few of those who represent the people have a strong interest in the overall health of the nation. At the state level, those who represent districts are often more concerned about what they believe is best for their district rather than what is best for the state. At the national level, those sent to congress are often more concerned with bringing home the bacon to their state than making decisions that are best for the nation as a whole. I believe this is one reason our nation is so heavily in debt. Our representatives have voted for programs they believe their constituents want without concerning themselves with how the programs are paid for. Once a government program is implemented it is extremely hard to eliminate even if it is obsolete.

Perhaps there needs to be a constitutional amendment that deals with the debt issue. Some have advocated a balanced budget amendment, but this may be too constrictive, in times of war for example. It will take someone a lot smarter than me to come up with acceptable wording for such an amendment that would actually force us to reduce our debt while providing for all contingencies. Unfortunately, the general public has become so accustomed to debt that most citizens seem to think it is no big deal.

It is not surprising that our legislators act the way they do. We as citizens tend to vote for representatives who promise tangible results for the state or district they represent. We tend to vote for what we want without thinking much about what is best for us. We also tend to vote based on name recognition rather than on actual analysis of a candidate's position on issues. This often results in the election of the candidate who spends the most money on advertising or the one who makes the most promises they know they cannot keep. Once in office, an incumbent has tremendous advantage over would-be opponents at least partly because name recognition can be enhanced through free mailings (franking privilege) and other means.

Recently during the 2016 primary election coverage on television I watched a reporter interview a citizen and ask which candidate she intended to vote for. She responded that she would vote for the candidate that was ahead in the polls, her argument being that she did not want to "waste her vote." While I was dumbfounded by such a response, I had certainly heard similar arguments before. I suppose people tend to naturally want to be on the winning side. But it seems to me that a person is indeed wasting her vote if she doesn't examine the issues and vote for the candidate who she believes is the most likely to best represent the national interest regardless of who is ahead in the polls. If polling has such a strong influence on how people vote, perhaps polling should be banned. After all, the news media does not project election results until after the polls close, supposedly in order not to influence voters. Perhaps the same reasoning could be extended to pre-election polling.

There are many things our government could do that would help achieve a sustainable future. Getting our fiscal house in order should be top priority and seems to me that it is essential from an economic point of view. Working toward a growth-neutral stance on population and economic matters seems just as important from an ecological point of view.

CHAPTER 12

FINAL THOUGHTS

At this point, I hope to have convinced the reader that economic growth is not sustainable over the long term, or at least I hope I have presented a logical argument that will generate some serious discussion and questioning of the currently prevailing wisdom concerning growth. If so, I would encourage you to bring up the subject of growth with your friends and perhaps let your community leaders know that you are concerned about the future quality of life that unchecked growth is likely to bring.

Perhaps a starting point would be to ask that growth not be encouraged by government policy and that growth should pay its own way. I have had considerable success in getting editorials published in several newspapers pointing out my views about the unsustainability of growth. I have gotten nothing but positive comments from readers of such editorials (mostly people who know me), but I have at times felt like a voice crying in the wilderness because the "grow or die" paradigm is so firmly entrenched and few other people seem willing to speak out.

If you have read this far, you have probably been thinking about whether or not you have your own personal financial interest in growth. Perhaps you are a homeowner who is counting on growth to drive up the value of your home so that you can make a substantial profit when you sell it. Perhaps you are a farmer who recognizes that your farm will ultimately be worth more to a developer than to a farmer. Or perhaps you own some undeveloped land or other real estate that is likely to increase in value as a result of growth.

On the other hand, maybe you are like the majority of citizens who own no property but live in a rented house or apartment where you have noticed that your rent keeps rising as population growth increases demand for rental property. If you have limited job skills perhaps you have noticed the increasing competition for low-paying jobs as technology has taken over repetitive tasks. Regardless of whether you own property or pay rent, growth drives up the cost of living. Even if you sell property for the profit that growth made possible you are likely to find that growth has also driven up the cost of any replacement property you may want to buy.

There are many reasons other than financial that a person might see growth as beneficial to his or her community. Growth in rural areas for example may result in more varied opportunities for nearby shopping and entertainment. Growth in such areas may also improve local job choices for young people moving into the work force and thus help keep families from being scattered to the four winds. These are all legitimate reasons for wanting growth in sparsely populated areas, but even in such situations I believe it is important for residents to be thinking about how much growth is good and what long term population density would be most desirable.

The prevailing wisdom is that economic growth increases opportunities for all and therefore has the potential for raising everyone's standard of living. But in actuality, growth has disproportionally benefited the wealthy as both income and wealth inequality have continued to escalate with rising GDP. I believe it is time for all of us to ask ourselves some hard questions about growth.

Are you in favor of economic growth that is supported by population growth? If so, how much do you think the population should grow in your city, county, or state before it reaches an optimum density? Do you believe that density doesn't matter and the population should keep growing forever? Is this realistic?

Are you in favor of economic growth that depends on the continued use of fossil fuels to make it happen? If so, what do you think life will be like for future generations once these fuels are exhausted? Do you think sufficient renewable fuel sources can be developed that will enable growth to continue forever?

Do you favor economic growth that depends on ever-increasing debt? Are you concerned about the possibility of national bankruptcy or massive inflation as a means of dealing with debt? Are you comfortable with passing debt to future generations so that the current population can live in largess?

Are you in favor of economic growth that swallows up farm and forest land and turns it into highly congested areas crammed with roads, buildings, concrete, and asphalt? How far should this trend go before you would think it has gone far enough? How far can it go before the earth's capability to supply food and building materials can no longer meet the needs of the growing population?

Are you in favor of economic growth that continues to increase income inequality? If so, what should society do to assist the increasing numbers of people who are unable to find a job where they can make a living wage? Do you believe that such people should receive public assistance or should they have to depend on private charity to survive? Do you care if they survive?

Regardless of whether you have an interest in growth, I hope you will support the preservation of green space in your community and the setting aside of undeveloped land for the public good. Properly maintained green space has many benefits, especially in areas of high population density. Environmental benefits of green space include air and water quality protection, temperature modification, and oxygen generation. Perhaps more important, green space benefits human health by providing places for increased physical activity to reduce stress and prevent obesity. Such areas also give city dwellers an opportunity to reconnect with nature and provide a temporary respite from busy lifestyles. Unfortunately, many communities come to realize the need for undeveloped areas only after much of the remaining suitable land has become too expensive to purchase with scarce public funds.

I have used the term optimum as it relates to both animal and human populations. But how does one determine what an optimum human population should be for a given area? I will be the first to admit that there is no easy answer to such a question, but I believe it is nevertheless a question that needs to be seriously considered. One way to think about this is to compare the political jurisdiction (city, county, parish, etc.) where you live with other nearby more densely populated areas. Ask yourself if you want the traffic congestion, the lack of parks and open spaces or the air or water quality problems you see in a nearby county. I have often heard people in the county where I live say that we don't want our county to be like the faster growing and congested county to the south, but our elected county and city commissioners continue to maintain the same policies that encourage the same kind of population growth and urban sprawl that has occurred in the county we don't want to be like.

Part of the problem with dealing with growth issues is that there is typically no serious discussion of what citizens want in the way of long-term planning. So-called comprehensive plans that may be devised by local governments are based largely on projections of future populations and zoning for different land uses. Population projections are based on past growth rates, which are likely to have been boosted by policies that encouraged growth. Citizens who question the wisdom of growth policies need not accept the typical response from elected officials that "growth is going to occur whether we want it or not" when it is clear that those officials are doing everything they can to gener-

ate more growth. Zoning is often used as a way of directing where different types of growth take place but I have
observed that zoning is easily changed to accommodate the
landowner's wishes to develop the property and thus is a
rather ineffective means of limiting growth.

Long-term planning needs to be driven by citizen
involvement, but many citizens who would like to discourage growth may be hesitant to get involved because
they believe that most people and certainly their elected
representatives consider growth inevitable. I have already
pointed out that long-term planning for most elected officials seems to go about as far into the future as the next
election cycle. Many politicians seem to be more interested
in getting re-elected than in paying serious attention to
citizens who question perpetual growth. After all, officials
generally have the backing of the urban growth machine I
mentioned in chapter 7 in order to get elected in the first
place and need the machine's support to stay in office.

Going back to the issue of optimum population,
this subject can be considered in a number of ways. One
way to think about it is in the context of available natural
resources that we all depend on. I hope I have made a good
argument that most of these resources are being used at an
unsustainable rate, so in that context it would seem that
optimum population density cannot be achieved in many
high-density areas unless there are fewer people or less use
of resources by the current population.

Another way of considering optimum population is in
terms of quality of life issues other than how much resources
we consume. Higher population density generally means

more government regulations and a larger bureaucracy to administer those regulations, aka bigger government. Bigger government generally means higher taxes (or more debt) and more restrictions on individual freedoms. Higher population density also means more money is needed to build, maintain, and upgrade or replace infrastructure. It also means less green space per capita, poorer water quality in streams and lower air quality which may seriously affect the ability of many citizens to breath.

If you are eligible to vote then by all means do so. When it comes to growth issues, there may be little choice among the candidates because most have bought into the growth equals progress paradigm and do not question the wisdom of perpetual growth. However, I believe that one should not be a single-issue voter, that is one who backs a candidate based on his stand on a single issue, a promise to create jobs, for example. Rather, please take the time to evaluate each candidate's position on a variety of issues and select the person who you think would do the best job of addressing the most serious problems. You might also ask yourself which candidate is most likely to be open-minded and thus be willing to listen and consider citizen input once elected. Has the candidate identified specific issues that need to be addressed and presented specific plans to deal with those issues?

Be careful not to let partisan politics cloud your judgment, especially on matters related to science. The subject of global warming is a good example of a science issue that has been turned into a political one. Many people refuse to believe in global warming because they fear that the economy will be hurt if steps are taken to curb carbon dioxide emissions or simply because they have heard someone they believe in call it a hoax. Even if you are not a scientist make an effort to understand the facts about important science issues. Scientists are by training skeptical, and you should also be skeptical, but pay attention when the vast majority of scientists seem to agree on an important issue.

Whatever you do, don't blindly vote for the candidate who is reported to be leading in the polls just because you believe he or she is the most likely to win and you have a desire to be on the winning side. In my opinion you are simply wasting your vote and ignoring your civic duty if you depend on the media polls to tell you how to vote. Keep in mind that many if not most politicians tell you what they think you want to hear rather than present a logical argument for solving problems. Again, be skeptical.

Personally, I consider myself an independent voter, one who owes no allegiance to any political party. Far too many politicians seem to put the interest of their party (and winning votes) ahead of solving the nation's problems. If this were not true, I believe our nation would not be so far in debt and our infrastructure would not be so dilapidated. These are problems that could easily be solved if our representatives in Washington or in our state capitals took them seriously and worked together to solve them in a fair and logical manner without worrying about who got the credit.

Consider the nation's deteriorating infrastructure (roads, bridges, etc.) as an example of a problem for which there is a logical solution known as "user pays." This is simply a matter of charging those who use the nation's roads and bridges, for example, enough money to pay for repairs. This has traditionally been accomplished by way of a per gallon fuel tax, but as vehicles get more fuel efficient the amount of tax money collected compared to the need has declined. A problem easily solved by raising the fuel tax. Electric vehicles could contribute to infrastructure repairs via a tax on the vehicles themselves and on replacement batteries. This is an example of a problem easily solved by statesmen, but difficult for politicians who fear being booted out of office if they vote to raise taxes, even when the tax money clearly benefits the majority of their constituents.

A business that measures success based on gross sales but makes no effort to determine net profits is quite likely to fail. By the same logic economists need a way to measure net economic well-being as opposed to depending on the gross value of goods and services to measure success. Some things to consider in measuring success could include such things as whether the amount of debt is increasing or decreasing, the status of infrastructure repair needs, whether aquifers are being replenished as fast as they are being drained and whether other natural resources are being used in a sustainable manner. The current system of measuring economic success based on GDP growth is deceptive in that it falsely portrays a growing economy as healthy even though it is not sustainable for future generations. From an ecological standpoint, GDP could just as logically stand for *gross deceptive product*.

It is beyond the scope of this book to make a prediction about how long economic growth can last or whether the economy will eventually collapse or just stagnate. There are too many variables involved and too many uncertainties to make any such predictions meaningful. I will leave it to the reader to thoughtfully consider the arguments I have made and if the reader wishes to make predictions so be it. Predictions or not, consider the possible consequences that are likely unless a steady state economy that works for all can be achieved.

In baseball, it's traditional that the visiting team is at bat during the first half of each inning and the home team bats last and thus has the last chance to win the game if it is behind in the score. In life, Nature (our ecosystem) is the home team that nourishes and sustains us all. Remember, no matter how much we humans alter our environment or develop our economies, in the long run nature's ecosystem, not the human economy, will determine our fate as a species.

To borrow a phrase coined by others: *Nature bats last.*

LITERATURE CITED

Carson, Rachael. 1962. *Silent Spring*. Houghton Mifflin.

Central Intelligence Agency. 2013. *The World Factbook (2013–2014)*. Washington, DC.

Federal Reserve System Board of Governors. 2017. "Changes in U.S. Family Finances Froom 2013 to 2016: Evidence From the Consumer Survey of Family Finances." Federal Reserve Bulletin. Vol. 103, No. 3.

Fodor, Eben. 2007. *Better not Bigger*. New Catalyst Books.

Hooke, Roger LeB., Jose F. Martin-Duque, and Javier Pedraza. "Land Transformation by Humans: A Review." *GSA Today*. 22(2012): 4-10.

Morris, Kenneth M. and Virginia B. 1999. *The Wall Street Journal Guide to Understanding Money & Investing*. The Lightbulb Press.

Smith, Adam. 1776. "An Inquiry Into the Nature and Causes of the Wealth of Nations." (As summarized in Wikipedia articles).

United Nation's World Commission on Environment and Development (Brundtland Commission). 1987. "Our Common Future."

US Department of Agriculture. 2013. Summary Report: 2010 National Resources Inventory, Natural Resources Conservation Service, Washington, DC, and Center for Survey Statistics and Methodology, Iowa State University, Ames, Iowa.

ABOUT THE AUTHOR

Russell England is a retired biologist and a master gardener. He has written numerous articles and opinion columns for various magazines and newspapers. He lives in Gainesville, Georgia, with his wife Pat.

CPSIA information can be obtained
at www.ICGtesting.com
Printed in the USA
LVHW041522221218
601135LV00001B/59/P

9 781640 037892